POWER IN STILLNESS

JERRI WOOD

Power in Stillness
Copyright © 2023 by Jerri Wood

ISBN:
Paperback: 979-8-9867725-8-5
e-book: 979-8-9867725-9-2

Riverview Press

info@riverview-press.com
www.riverview-press.com

Be Still

The first part of Psalm 46:10 says, "Be still." It is hoped that as you read through each chapter you will be able to see the need to be still before God and allow Him to do a work in your life.

In this section we will look at worry and what it does in our lives, letting Jesus calm any storm you may be going through, fear in our lives, ways to study and get God's Word in our hearts and understanding how much God really loves us. Power lies in understanding all these things and growing in God's grace.

And Know

The second section of this book is all about getting to know Jesus. It's about who He is, why He is the One to follow, and how to get to know Him, to accept Him and follow Him. The intention of this section is to help yourself or others get to know Jesus.

That I am God

The last section is about God's Omnipotence, His Omnipresence, and His Omniscience. Once we understand these things, we can truly start worshipping Him for how great He really is.

It is my hope that you, the reader, can gain a deeper knowledge of our Father, His Son and the Holy Spirit. I pray you take something you learn here and find a way to implement it into your life and grow closer to Jesus.

Acknowledgement

To all the ladies who gave me encouragement along the way:
My sister Judy who read for me and encouraged me.

The ladies in my Bible study group, for believing in me from the start.

To Rosemary, my new author friend, for graciously giving me encouragement.

To my daughter Stephanie who helped me with the cover and all the technical issues.

To my friend Joy who allowed us to share in her testimony.

To Pat who helped me edit this book.

To my friend Aileen Jacobs for supplying the prayers at the end of each chapter.

To my husband for letting me go on and on about my writing.

Thank you all for your support.

Dedication

To all my encouragers! You know who you are!

Summary

This book is written using the verse from Psalm 46:10, Be still and know that I am God. (Today's New International Version). It is broken up into three parts. "Be still"; "And know"; and "That I am God." Each section can stand alone or the entire book could be used as a Bible study. It is hopeful that it will bring the reader into a closer relationship with God, by gaining a better understanding of His Word, leading others to Christ, and learning that God is amazing!

Be Still

Chapter 1

Fret Not

Have you ever found yourself worrying over every little thing? Do you find it hard to stop worrying once you get going? I just want you to know you are not alone. I think if we're being honest, we would have to admit we worry about things all the time. I have found a scripture that I think will help with this problem. It is found in Psalm 37:1-11 and verses 27 and 34 (Today's New International Version) from the same chapter.

I feel like this topic is something we all need to hear about and I would guess we all struggle with it as well. What are some things that you are worrying about: financial issues, how about your kids, the washing machine, the dog, the car that's broken down, troubles on the job, needing a job? I think you get the picture! It doesn't matter how many people might be in a room, there would be that many different things folks would worry about.

So, I believe that Psalm 37 repeats the phrase "fret not", because it is, first of all, very important to be worry free, and second, it seems that everyone is worrying about something!

In the Bible when something is repeated, that means the phrase or word is important. So, why is it important to be worry free? Just think for a moment about the physical and emotional illnesses brought on by worrying or fretting. Here is a list of just a few: muscle tension, headaches, insomnia, depression, high blood pressure, increased risk of diabetes, heart disease, weakened immune system, ulcers, acid reflux, panic attacks, IBS, arthritis, migraines. And the list could go on and on. Isn't that a scary thought?

Do you have any of these things going on in your life? Is it brought on by worry? I want you to think about the things happening in your life right now. Write down whatever that stressful situation is somewhere, maybe even in the margin on this page. I'd like you to be able to refer back to it after we finish this chapter.

Let's get started with verse 1 in Psalm 37. In Bible studies I lead, I always tell ladies to use your dictionaries! You may think you know what a word means, but sometimes there is a new twist that just might make you sit up and take notice.

Alright, back to verse one. "Do not fret because of those who are evil, or be envious of those who do wrong." (Today's New International Version). By the way, Proverbs 24:19 is almost identical to this verse. Isn't it amazing how God inspired writers to write similar things, sometimes years apart? In this verse the connotation for fret is that there is anger involved. We will discuss this anger issue later. I see something else in this verse as well.

Let's look at that word "fret". The Greek words for fret mean, "to worry, or to divide the mind." [1] That is exactly what is happening to you when you worry over something. Your mind is divided or maybe it even feels lopsided because you spend the majority of your time thinking about THAT thing! If that doesn't give you a clear picture, how about this: "to eat away at, gnaw, it is an irritation, annoyance, or discontentment." [2]

Now think about your mind when you are worrying or fretting over something. Is it eating away at you? Is it a discontentment? Here is another mental picture for you. A "fret" is also "an ornamental net or network worn as a headdress." [3] It intersects at right angles. Fretting sets our minds going in this pattern (think Tic Tac Toe board or hashtag) and we lose sight of what our great God is able to do for us. Is it any wonder we find ourselves going crazy or having symptoms of some of those diseases listed earlier? By the way, did you notice the word disease can be broken into two words, dis ease?

There is a reason they are called that. We are at dis ease when we worry or fret. I don't know about you, but I want to get off that merry go round or square-dancing board and find out how to get better at handling stress and worry.

Me telling you not to fret or even the Bible telling you not to doesn't make the thing worrying you go away, does it? It is so easy to talk about, but soooo hard to do. I think if we look at some more verses in Psalm 37, we will see that God has given us a plan, a blueprint if you will. I think He wants to help us learn to "be still" and stop worrying. Verse three says, "Trust in the LORD and do good, dwell in the land and enjoy safe pasture." (New American Standard Bible). One version says, "cultivate faithfulness". (Berean Standard Bible). I love that and will come back to it in a bit.

First, this verse tells us to trust in the LORD. The definition of trust is, "an assured reliance on the character, ability, strength or truth of someone or something."[4] So let me ask you, where do you put your trust? Are you putting your trust in Jesus' reliability, his ability and strength, or are you trying to fix your problem on your own? That is our temptation, isn't it? To think that we are more than capable to fix problems that come up in our lives. After all, God gave us good minds, we should be able to do this, to figure out a solution to this problem. Well, I'm here to tell you there are times when there are no answers. Sometimes God has to work in another person's heart before the answer will be forthcoming. Sometimes God has to work in my heart and your heart before things get fixed.

There are a couple of other words in verse one I want to look at as well. The next word in that verse that I want to explore is "dwell". You know what I'm going to say - let's look at the definition! To dwell is a verb that means to live somewhere, to reside, hang out, or hang one's hat. Okay, some of those are my definitions of that word!

When I think of dwelling in the land like our verse says, I believe it means we need to hang out with God. Be still and spend some time talking to Him and listening to Him. Listen for His voice. You know the one. That voice that you hear when you are in worship of Him and in awe of Him. Hang out with Him. He is the one with the answers, so shouldn't we go to Him to gain His wisdom?

Living *for* God is different than living *with* Him. When you live for God, He is the recipient of your desire or activities, when you live with God, you are in a relationship with Him, and that is what He desires. Do you see the difference? The first one is your desire, the second is His desire.

The next phrase from verse 3 we want to focus on is the phrase, "cultivate faithfulness". Cultivate always sounds like a farming word to me and it can be, but here is the definition: "to improve by care, training, or study, to acquire or develop (a quality, sentiment or skill)."[5]

Studying God's word, training yourself in what the Bible has to say, acquiring the skills you need to get through each hour, sometimes each moment, are important things to do. Cultivate God's Word in your life. Again, spend time in His presence, listen to His voice, give care to studying His Word. Listen to worship music, pray. Most of all "be still".

Remember the whole point of this chapter is to help you stop fretting! God is giving us a blue- print here. If we can apply these things in our lives, I think we will be feeling much better about our situations.

I must stop here and tell you what is happening during the writing of this chapter! It all started with a leak under our kitchen sink. My husband, who has done some plumbing work while working with a construction crew, got under the sink and tightened up some things. About a week or so later, I noticed water under the sink again and the water was really slow to drain. Of course, we tried a drain declogger thinking that there must be a clog somewhere.

Then the garbage disposal stopped working! So, we replaced the disposal and all seemed well, until we tried running the dishwasher.

It would run for a few minutes then stop and say there was a clog somewhere. We found out that the new disposal had a plug that must be taken out, so after that was taken care of, the dishwasher started working. Yeah! Nope, not done yet!

You have to understand that everything had to be out from under the sink, and the dishwasher was out from under the cabinet. My kitchen was a mess! Thinking everything was fixed we were happy, but then our plumbing sprang another leak closer to the floor and started leaking into the living room as well as the kitchen. Then because the water had to be turned off, the washing machine wouldn't work! AAAAHHHH! No fretting going on for this lady, huh uh!

During this time, (we are about two weeks into this or so), my husband started having to work mandatory overtime, going in at 4:30 am, my sister-in-law's car broke down, and we were helping to take care of our daughter's place while she was away for the weekend!

My husband finally got a free moment to work on our leaking problem. He thought he had it fixed. He worked really hard on it too, but the minute we turned the water back on, we had a fountain flowing onto the kitchen floor. This happened not once, but twice, when I finally said, "Honey, call the plumber!" You see it wasn't that my husband didn't know how to fix the problem, because he did. The problem was that he didn't have all the information he needed. We found out from the plumber that there is a type of piping that is stronger that has to be used in the type of house where we live. You see we needed to have the correct information to make the repair. Are you seeing a correlation here?

Without our Father's help, we aren't strong enough either. If we spend time with Him and get His word tucked away in our hearts, then when things come along that shake us up, we can still be victorious. Was I perfect through all of this? NO! Was I better because I spent time with Jesus during all this mess? YES! I can tell you I did a lot of praying over that sink! Oh the lessons we can learn!

There were several things God gave me during this time. One of my daily devotions from Sarah Young's book, *Jesus Calling* said this: "Stop and affirm trust in God. Calmly bring matters to Him. Leave them in His hands, then simply do the next thing. (My next thing, by the way, was mopping up the floor with towels). Stay in touch through thankful, trusting prayers, resting in His sovereign control. Rejoice in Him, exult in the God of my salvation."[6] I surely tried to do that during this adventure! I really did not fly off the handle or lose my temper or do anything that you might expect and I have to attribute that to God's supernatural power working in me.

Another thing God gave me was the passage in Habakkuk 3:17-19. "Though the fig tree does not bud and there are no grapes on the vines, though the olive crop fails, and the fields produce no food, though there are no sheep in the pen, and no cattle in the stalls, yet I will rejoice in the LORD, I will be joyful in God my Savior. The Sovereign LORD is my strength; he makes my feet like the feet of a deer; he enables me to tread on the heights." (New International Version). If you will indulge me a moment, I rewrote this to outline my situation.

Though the sink leaks, and the drain won't drain, though the garbage disposal shuts down and has to be replaced, though the dishwasher stops and the washer won't wash and almost every towel in the house is wet, yet I will rejoice in God who provides me with peace. God was my strength; He helped me wade through the waters till they all dried up!

I felt like this quote from Charles Stanley was very pertinent, "Apart from the supernatural involvement of God, all their self-effort was in vain."[7] You see, sometimes we just try to take care of things by ourselves when we should be entrusting them to God. He has all the answers anyway, so why not let Him? Okay, moving on!

The next verse we want to look at in Psalm 37 is verse four. "Delight yourself in the LORD and He will give you the desires of your heart." (Berean Study Bible). Delight when used as a noun means, "a high degree of pleasure or enjoyment."[8] If it's used as a verb though it gets even more interesting. Delight as a verb means, "to captivate or entrance!"[9] Are you entranced or captivated by the Lord? Are we so in a love relationship with Him that we are fascinated with what He does in our lives? Some other synonyms for captivate are, dazzle, enthrall, draw, gratify, intrigue. There are many more, but you get the picture. We need to be a fan of Jesus, but we also and more importantly need to be a follower! We need to be so in love with Him that we are captivated by His love for us. That takes stillness and quietness to find.

To this point we have looked at trusting in the Lord by cultivating our relationship with Him. We do this through worship, reading His Word, praying, being still and listening for His voice. Verse five and six is our next stop on our way to being "fret free".

"Commit your way to the Lord, trust in him and he will do this: He will make your righteous reward shine like the dawn, your vindication like the noon day sun." (New International Version). Think about a time you made a commitment. How did you feel? Could you turn it on and off like a light switch? Were you able to just walk away whenever you wanted a vacation?

I was an elementary school teacher and sometimes I felt like it was more trouble to get ready for a substitute teacher to come in for a day, or heaven forbid, for several days, than it was for me to just work when I was sick! I know that sounds ridiculous, but you see, I had a commitment to my job, the students, my boss and my co-workers, that needed to be fulfilled. I needed to make sure that those in my care were taken care of. People entrusted me to do a good job. Not to mention that the substitute needed to know what was going on in great detail!

So, my question is, are there things we need to be doing when we've committed our way to the Lord? Matthew 22:37-38 says we are to "Love the Lord our God with all our heart, and with all our soul, and with all our mind."(New International Version). That sounds like a complete package to me. I asked the question on gotquestions.org, "What does the Bible say about commitment?"

Here was the answer and I think it's a good one. "Total commitment to God means that Jesus is our sole authority, our guiding light and our unerring Compass. Being committed to Christ means being fruitful; it means being a servant."[10] Is He your sole authority, the One you go to for help and answers? Is He your Guiding Light when you don't know which way to turn, and your Compass when you don't know which way to go? I sure hope you can say with confidence that He is!

We've looked at trusting in the Lord, delighting in the Lord and committing our way to the Lord. Let's see what verse seven has for us. "Be still before the Lord and wait patiently for Him, do not fret when men prosper in their way, when they carry out wicked schemes."(Berean Study Bible). It seems we've come full circle. Be still and wait patiently. I want to take a moment right now and have you do something. Set the stopwatch on your phone for two minutes. Then, I just want you to sit in silence till the alarm goes off. Focus on God during this time. Just be still. After the two minutes are up, return back to the rest of this chapter.

Did you find it hard to be still? Were you able to focus on God and see what He might be saying? The next time you might make it a little longer. Sometimes you just have to wait to see when God will speak, but oh, when He does, it will be well worth it!

On to verse eight where we see another directive at work in our blueprint for being still and not fretting. "Refrain (cease) from anger and abandon wrath; do not fret, it can only bring harm (it only leads to evil). (Berean Study Bible). I got a chuckle when I looked up 'The Message' translation for this verse. Here is what it says: "Bridle your anger, trash your wrath, cool your pipes (The Message Bible) - it only makes things worse." Don't you love that wording? "Cool your pipes!" As funny as that may sound, it seems there is a direct correlation between being angry and not fretting. Think about that situation you wrote down at the beginning of this chapter. Do you find that there was some friction that caused your worry? Anything in that problem that rubbed you the wrong way? That teenager not living up to what you thought they should? Your co-worker sloughing off and you have to pick up the slack? It could be anything that causes you to be angry, but you see, if we don't "cool our pipes", we won't be able to be still and even worse, when we fret about it, the verse says it leads to evil! We don't want to go there!

Verse 27 brings us to the next point. It tells us to "Turn away from evil and do good, so that you will abide forever." (Berean Study Bible). When you turn from something, you reverse the course of it. You stop or repel that thing. Think about a raincoat- it repels the water so you don't get wet. This verse is telling us to be a raincoat from evil. Turn it away, repel it, don't let it soak in. Ephesians 4:27 says, "And do not give the devil a foothold."(Berean Study Bible). In other words, don't give the devil a chance to start something. Stop him in his tracks before he gets started. Don't listen to him. Fill your mind with God's word, get scripture in there that will give you the strength you need to get through this next problem.

In verse 27 we see the word, abide. One version says, we will "live securely"[11] The Latin for secure is broken up this way; SE- without, CURE- Care. So put together, secure means to be free from care. If we turn from evil like water does off a duck's back, then we can live without care, doubt, anxiety (NO FRETTING). I want to live this free! I know you do too!

One last word on the subject of not fretting. Verse 34 tells us to "Wait for the LORD and keep his way, and He will raise you up to inherit the land." (Berean Study Bible). Again, we are looking at that word, WAIT! The definition of the word is, "to stay where one is or delay action until a particular time or, (and I love this part), until something else happens!"[12]

Think about that for a minute. If we were to wait for the Lord until something else happened, until He spoke or moved or fixed the problem, what would that look like? Would we see some awesome miracles? Would there be some lives changed because we waited?

In short, there are several things we need to do: Trust God, delight in Him, commit our ways to Him, be still, cool our pipes and turn away from evil and wait on God. Remember that situation you wrote down earlier in this chapter? I'd like you to look at it again. Can you trust God with it? Will you allow yourself to be delighted by Jesus? Let yourself rest in Him and be patient. Wait on God to work in this situation. Hear from Him and allow Him to work. You won't be sorry.

As I let go of all that I worry about, may I learn to leave it all with You. It is human nature to want to take back those things I fret about. I trust that You have me covered in Your love, grace and peace. Today, I leave my cares in Your hands as the One who keeps me from fret and worry.

Your Name be blessed.

Amen.

Section 1

Chapter 2

Be Still

When I think of being still there is one word that I feel like we need to focus on. That word is peace. There are a lot of scriptures that refer to peace, but I want to focus on a particular passage. You will find it in Mark 4:35-41. This is the story about Jesus calming the storm. If you are not familiar with the story here it is:

"That day when evening came, he said to his disciples, 'Let us go over to the other side.'

Leaving the crowd behind, they took him along, just as he was, in the boat. There were also other boats with him. A furious squall came up and the waves broke over the boat so that it was nearly swamped. Jesus was in the stern, sleeping on a cushion. The disciples woke him and said to him, "Teacher, don't you care if we drown?"

He got up, rebuked the wind and said to the waves, "Quiet! Be Still!" Then the wind died down and it was completely calm.

He said to his disciples, "Why are you so afraid? Do you still have no faith?"

They were terrified and asked each other, "Who is this? Even the wind and the waves obey him!" (New International Version).

Matthew 8:23-27 is the same story, but I love the way Matthew puts the question when the disciples speak. They asked, "What kind of man is this?" (New International Version). This got me to thinking. Just what kind of man is Jesus to me? Have you ever thought about Him like that?

I could spend a whole book or two or three telling what kind of man Jesus is, but I just picked out some things I want to discuss. Just like Jesus calmed the physical storm in the story, He can calm the storms in your life too! What might you be going through? Do you need His peace? Do you find yourself feeling like the disciples did, "Lord, save me?" He can take whatever that storm is and calm it down to peace.

First Peter 1:6-7 says, "Trials come so that our faith can be proved genuine and will result in glory to God."(New International Version). Ugh! Trials are tough! I don't like them either, but they are necessary for our growth. If you never went through a hard time, how would you know if you could endure it? How would you ever be able to see God's saving hand working in your life?

When I taught elementary school, one of my favorite subjects to teach was science. One of the things we studied about was rocks. Metamorphic rocks are formed when "rocks are subjected to high heat, high pressure, hot mineral-rich fluids or, more commonly, some combination of these factors." (usgs.gov).[13]

Just like metamorphic rocks become tough when heat and pressure or a combination of those things are applied, so do we, when we encounter adversity. I tend to collect sayings and short blurbs that have meaning to me. I heard this one at a conference and never forgot it. "A stream with no rocks makes no music." Another one is, "You'll never know that God is all you need, till God is all you've got!"

I think both of these sayings are very pertinent. Until we have been tested, until some tough situation comes along, we might miss the fact that we need Jesus to get in our boat and calm the storm! I tend to see God more fully when there are difficult times going on in my life. If you are honest, I believe you do too!

Philippians 4:6-7 says, "Do not be anxious about anything, but in every situation, by prayer and petition, with thanksgiving, present your requests to God. And the peace of God which transcends all understanding, will guard your heart and your minds in Christ Jesus."(New International Version).

First, God says, "Do not be anxious!" What? I'm not supposed to be anxious or worried, or afraid? How can I not be? We know the disciples were afraid of the mighty storm that was overtaking them or Jesus wouldn't have asked them why they were still so afraid. I don't think we are any different than the disciples. We become afraid too, but let's look at the second part of that verse. "But in every situation by prayer and petition with thanksgiving, present your requests to God." It is wonderful to have a God who we can go to, who will take our hurts, who knows what we need before we do. Don't be anxious. Take your fears, your hard times, your worries to Him and ask for His help. While you are asking, don't forget to thank Him and praise Him for the life He's given you, for keeping you from evil. Thank Him for the small stuff: a pretty day, a flower, your home. Thank Him for salvation and for just being God! I believe when we thank Him our attitude starts to change. I think we start to trust God more. Put your trust in Jesus, that He will change this hard time you're going through into something amazing!

The next verse, verse seven, gives us the results. Once we have prayed to God about what is going on and thanked Him, we get the best part ever! He gives us peace that passes our understanding. Ephesians 2:14 says, "For he himself is our peace."(NIV). That is Jesus being spoken of there. He is our peace! Just like he calmed that storm with the words, "Peace! Be still!" I believe He wants us to be at peace, to be still and let Him take care of those storms for us.

James 1:2-4 says: "Consider it pure joy, my brothers and sisters, whenever you face trials of many kinds, because you know that the testing of your faith produces perseverance. Let perseverance finish its work so that you may be mature and complete, not lacking anything." (NIV). Webster's dictionary defines perseverance as; "continued effort to do or achieve something despite difficulties, failure or opposition."[14] That sounds like the Christian life to me. In our lives as Christians, we will continue to become more like Jesus, even though we go through difficult times. We may experience failure and we will have lots of opposition in the world. Jesus himself said we would have difficulties and troubles in this life.

Without trials, hard times, and tests, our faith won't be able to mature. Perseverance is work. It's a continual effort to achieve God's final work in our lives. God wants us to be strong in Him. He wants up to grow up and be mature and complete.

One other thing stands out to me in this story. Did you notice that Jesus was asleep in the boat? If you notice in the first part of that story in Mark 4:36 it says, "Leaving the crowd behind, they (the disciples) took him along, just as he was, in the boat."(NIV). That phrase, just as he was, caught my attention. He was exhausted, worn out, tired. But again, here's the important part. He was asleep! He wasn't on deck wringing his hands. He wasn't worrying about the boat sinking. He was asleep! Yeah, I know you are thinking, but He was Jesus! Of course, he wasn't afraid, and you are right. He is the Master of the Sea. I don't know about you, but I take great comfort in knowing the Master of the Sea! That very same Jesus who calmed that storm is available to us as well.

A friend of mine at church went through rough seas and as I was writing this chapter, I asked her if she would mind giving me her testimony for this book. She agreed and I'm going to tell it in her words to do it justice. After all, she was the one who lived it! So here is Joy's story.

"In 2014, it became clear that my amazing, God - loving husband had a devastating dementia problem, one that would ultimately take his life in 2019, at 70 years of age. After Jim was diagnosed with early onset Alzheimer's, all our thoughts and prayers naturally centered on how to prepare, to cope and survive. Was our God big enough? Could we trust Him with even this? I soon began to sense that the Lord wanted us to move from our beloved country home of 34 years in central Illinois, to Columbia, MO, where we would be closer to our three daughters. I prayed about this for months--" Lord, I do love my Missouri and Kansas kids and grandkids, but is it not enough that I am losing my rock, my dearest friend to this horrible disease? Am I to understand that you want us to also leave our cherished home, our lifelong friends, our church, our lives?" I am not going to lie, there was worry, fear, panic, and many tears. Our son, an EMT, his sweet wife, a nurse practitioner, and their children lived nearby. "It would make no sense to move away from that love and support, right, Lord? I must be misunderstanding!" Although I was feeling windswept and battered, the Lord continued to speak His love into my life. His written Word became my lifeline. Isaiah 41:9-10 "You are my servant. For I have chosen you and will not throw you away. Don't be afraid for I am with you. Don't be discouraged for I am your God. I will strengthen you and help you. I will hold you up with my righteous right hand." "Yes, Lord, but surely such a move would be simply too much to ask of a person already struggling with serious memory loss and confusion." I finally mentioned to our son that I was feeling the Lord calling us to somehow move to Columbia. In shocked surprise, he said he and our daughter-in-law had been praying about it for months! Emboldened, I shared the growing impression with our closest friends. Like me, they were saddened by the thought, but they agreed to pray with me and trust the Lord to make a way, if indeed it was meant to happen. Finally, one morning, I just asked Jim about it. Wouldn't you know, after I had wrestled with the dilemma for months, Jim (the man struggling with dementia) came to me the following morning and simply said, "We should move to Missouri." Now I stared in shocked surprise and, just like that, it was decided. "But how in the world do we accomplish this, Lord?" became my plea. Matthew 11:28 promises, "Come to me, all you who are weary and burdened, and I will give you rest." God's assurance and love was my oxygen during this season. In early 2015, our son's family together with Jim and I traveled to Columbia one weekend to see our Kansas grandkids compete in a swim meet. The entire family was in attendance and someone suggested that we check out some properties around Columbia that afternoon. That very day, the Lord directed us to the perfect home for our needs: ADA compliant, no steps at all, room for my live-in mom, and situated on 13 acres- enough acreage to provide a nice lot where our son could build a home for his family. Soon the deal was struck, and now the pressure was on to sell our home in Illinois. We spoke to realtors about listing the home and property, but I was not comfortable with their recommended selling price. Jim was no longer able to lead in these decisions, but my mustard seed of faith was on the rise now- I took my phone out to our front yard, snapped a photo and submitted my add to the local newspaper. For sale by Owner, at $75,000 above the realtor recommended price. In three days, it was sold, praise the Lord!

The five years between Jim's diagnosis in 2014, and his home-going in 2019, truly felt like a walk through the valley of death most days. There were countless obstacles, sorrows, confusion, many sleepless nights, and very scary moments, We, however, were never alone and His Presence surrounded us day and night. We lived out those days in the promises of Psalm 121 and discovered that indeed, God neither slumbers nor sleeps. The Lord provided absolutely everything and everyone we needed to walk that journey, including a wonderful new church and many new friends. As Jim's mind drifted away, I found comfort in knowing his spiritual battles were over, his soul was already safe in God's arms even as we struggled through the day to day. For me, I learned to trust the Lord more than ever before, to find rest in His love moment by moment. When I cried out to Jesus for help, He always delivered. He sent encouragers, people to pray, people to physically help. Our children and grandchildren were able to love on Jim (Pop to the grands) in a beautiful way- always bringing a smile to his face until the very end. I found great strength and hope in the written Word and have now filled a journal with His beloved promises.

Into that terrible storm, Jesus spoke, "Peace, be still. And the wind ceased, and there was a great calm." (American Standard Version).

He was in my friend's day-to-day, as well as her future. He is in your future! He knows what is going to happen. He knows your issues and your problems and mine too. Will I be like the people in the boat with Him, asking if He cares whether I am drowning or not? Of course, He cares! Let Him still those waves for you. He can make it happen. It may not be right away like it was on that lake, but He will calm the storm and give you peace. Be still and be quiet so you can feel His presence.

Just as Jesus came to teach and show us peace, You are there to teach us that, "We are weak, but You are strong." In these days of uncertainty and chaos, bring peace and calm the storms I am facing right now. Teach me to climb from the valley to the mountain top. I praise You and give You the glory!

Amen and Amen.

Chapter 3

Fear Not

It all started around July 22nd or 23rd or maybe a few days earlier. You see I didn't realize at the time that I would be writing about it, so I didn't keep track. That morning I had gotten up at my usual time, probably between 6-6:30 AM. It was just like any other morning. Fixed my coffee and my breakfast and proceeded to have my quiet time with the Lord. I want you to know that my times with Jesus have become so much better because I've been reading His Word, writing scripture, listening to music and just sitting quietly and listening for His voice. Sometimes He prompts me to write notes to people, or post something on Facebook, or to call someone, or even to bake brownies and take them to an older gentleman down the street! This day I didn't feel any particular leading and so I finished up my time.

Here is when it got really interesting. I had gotten dressed and was just putting on my shoes, when I heard God say, "I want you to write a book!" He even gave me a rough outline using a scripture that I had in the devotions that day. It was very distinct. Now, first of all, I have learned over the years that I have to be sure that this is God's voice I'm hearing. Second, I have never written a book before. As a matter of fact, I would consider myself a speaker/teacher, rather than a writer. I have felt for a long time that God was leading me into speaking for Him at retreats and other gatherings for women, not writing a book! Surprise!

So, when I even thought about writing a book, I can say there was fear. I can say there was doubt, awe, surely this can't be! I even told God, "Lord, you know I'm not a writer!" You see, I had a college professor who once told me that I was not a good writer. I guess I really took that to heart, because I focused on that one negative professor instead of focusing on all the other professors who had given me A's on writing assignments. That one negative thing outweighed all others. Anyway, God was not giving up on this. He just would not let this idea of a book get out of my head. So, I followed Priscilla Shirers' 5 M advice.

The first M in her model is Message: "Look for the Message of the Spirit. Look inside yourself and listen to how your conscience is responding."[15] My brain was saying I couldn't possibly, but my heart was saying, "You know this is what God wants." So, that led me to the second M.

The second M is: "Search the Model of scripture for guidance."[15] On July 24, I started to come across scriptures like Deuteronomy 31:8 "The LORD himself goes before you and will be with you; he will never leave you, nor forsake you. Do not be afraid; do not be discouraged."(New International Version). Another verse was Psalm 73:23. "Yet I am always with you; you hold me by my right hand." (NIV). Yet another was Isaiah 41:10. "So do not fear, for I am with you; do not be dismayed for I am your God. I will strengthen you and help you; I will uphold you with my righteous right hand."(NIV).

That same day my devotion in Sarah Young's book *Jesus Always,* started out with, "Do not be afraid; do not be discouraged. You are looking ahead at uncertainties, letting them unnerve you. Fear and discouragement are waiting alongside your pathway into the future-ready to accompany you if you let them. "Yet I am always with you, holding you by your right hand. Cling tightly to My hand and walk resolutely past those dark presences of fearfulness and despair."[16] Then she quoted Isaiah 41:10.

Here is the prayer I wrote in my journal that morning:

Oh Lord, thank you for Isaiah 41:10! I'm so glad that you are <u>always</u> there for me. You know, Lord, that I'm waiting and wanting confirmation about this book writing. I feel like today's devotion is a step in that direction. I am willing to give this my best, but I definitely need your help!

On to the third M which is Mode. "Live in the mode of prayer."[15] Believe me when I say that I did a lot of praying about this. I couldn't stop thinking about it and when I thought about it, I would find myself praying. I was able to bring it to Him and wait and look for confirmations to come or not, because I wasn't going to do this if it really wasn't what God wanted.

The next M is "Submit to the Ministry of Eli"[15]. This means to seek the counsel of a mature believer. I didn't share this with just everyone at first. I did however talk to my good friend at church. She was immediately all for it and even gave me the idea for a chapter on fear, which you are now reading. I felt that God had given me the outline for this book and one of the sections is called "Be Still."

All of these things were leading me to the fifth M. "Expect the Mercy of confirmation".[15] Not only did I have the scriptures I quoted earlier, but I went to church and we had a guest speaker. He preached about being on a journey, and how God is in our future, just like my devotional, and he used Isaiah 41:10 and Isaiah 40:31! Oh, my goodness!

I decided I needed to write this man a note (he is a member of our church) and tell him that what he preached was what I needed to hear! I told him about the use of the same verses, and how I felt like this was all a confirmation of things I'd been praying about! The awesome thing was, his wife told me later, he had gone off script! He didn't even preach what he had in his notes! It was exactly what I needed to hear and God knew that! He confirmed for me what I needed to know. When you ask for confirmation, stand firm and believe it will come. But God wasn't done yet!

Needless to say, I started to write. As I said before, I have always been a teacher/speaker and I've written lots of lessons for different occasions. I felt God prompting me to look at those lessons again, which I did. I was able to organize some of them to fit into my outline. Once I started writing it seemed like the words just flew right on to the page! What an experience for me who always felt that writing just wasn't my thing!

Here's another prayer I wrote in my journal. "Oh, Lord Jesus, Your word tells me you will direct me, teach me, guide me and counsel me in the way I need to go. I believe you are doing this very thing in my life right now. You know I sure wasn't even thinking of publishing a book I haven't even written yet, and yet You showed me that there are Christian publishers out there willing to help! I'm thrilled and a bit overwhelmed, but I believe that You are in this and you will guide me each step of the way.

Thank you for believing in me, help me to do my best for you. I feel like this will be your work not mine. Help me be an instrument of yours to work on this undertaking. Help me, Jesus, to be led by you."

Here is what happened. I was trying to find a certain book for use in our ladies Bible study and went directly to the publisher of the book. The first thing that came up, even before finding the book, was an ad for self-publishing! What?! I'm not even there in my thinking yet! Amazing that God was educating me about this before the need arose. I even dreamed about writing a book, probably because it had been on my mind so much, but it was a pleasant dream and that gave me a pick me up too!

There was one last confirmation from God that I must tell you about. I had gone to a new store in town that a friend of mine had just bought. I was telling her about God wanting me to write a book. She immediately reached out her hand and picked up a business card which she promptly handed to me. She said, "You need to contact this lady! She is a friend of mine and she just wrote her first book during COVID. You will like her and she can maybe be a good resource." Well, I thought that was pretty awesome, so a couple of days later, I did contact her. My friend was right! This woman couldn't have been any sweeter. We talked back and forth on Messenger for quite a long time and a new friendship was formed. I told her what I was doing and had just gotten started and asked her if she would be willing to read something I had written so far. She graciously agreed and her feedback was so complimentary that I got busy and wrote some more. I have also asked a few others to read for me too, and the feedback has been great. I just needed to know that what I was putting down on paper made sense to someone else.

Sometimes I feel presumptuous to even be thinking that I can do this task for God, but then He reminds me that if I just trust Him and listen and follow closely that I have nothing to fear. Here is another prayer I wrote in my journal:

"Lord, I see a promise that You are going to continue to help me with my book writing. You know I do feel presumptuous to be doing this. It is certainly out of my wheelhouse and yet You are making a way for me to do this. Thank you, Jesus, for your grace!"

The writing of this chapter is me facing my fear. God has literally written this chapter as I have lived it out. He has directed me to tell my story in this chapter as a way for you to know that you can face your fears too.

My verse this morning was Proverbs 16:3. "Commit to the LORD whatever you do and he will establish your plans."(NIV). When I looked this verse up in the concordance, I found that the Hebrew for the phrase "commit thy works unto the LORD means, "Roll unto the LORD" like a man rolls a burden to another because it's too heavy and he needs help. I so love that, because that's exactly what I feel like I've done. I rolled the writing of this book onto the Lord and let Him do it through me.

One last thing about the rest of Proverbs 16:3. Gills Exposition of the Entire Bible says this: "When a man (or in this case a woman) has, by faith and in prayer, committed himself, his case, his ways and works, to the Lord, his mind is made easy, his thoughts are composed and settled and he quietly waits the issue of things; he says the will of the Lord be done; he knows that He causes all things to work together for good."[17] My mind and my heart are easy after writing this chapter. His will be done.

I pray there is hope in this chapter for you somewhere. I pray you will see with the eyes of your heart that you can overcome your fear. You can do that thing that God is asking you to do. Don't let that opportunity go by. Trust Him to help you, lead you, and guide you. You can do this!

Father, I am listening today for Your instruction. I am trusting that it is Your will that I follow Your voice. Make real in me the path You want me to follow. I want to get out of the way, so that Your light shines and brings a calm retreat to Your people.

In the Name of Jesus,

Amen.

Chapter 4

Growing Peace through the Change

Metamorphosis is a big word that means there are changes in the form of an animal during its life cycle. We most often think of the butterfly when we use this word. You know, it starts out as an egg, that egg develops into larvae which is basically a worm or caterpillar, then when that caterpillar is full grown it will turn into the pupa or chrysalis stage. It may stay in this stage for many months, before it comes into the adult stage, which is what we know as a butterfly or a moth.

Wow! What a transformation. It looks nothing like it did when it started out as an egg! Do you ever look back on your life and consider how different you are now? I would say you've changed, hopefully for the better!

We as women also go through The Change! It is a dreaded word for some to even think about. You know that the word menopause is spelled that way for a reason, don't you? It's because men say, "O and pause!" It's not a good time to mess with a woman! I'm really just kidding here, because women are not the only ones who change. In the spiritual realm everyone who becomes a Christian should be going through a change, a growing process. If you aren't and you feel stuck in one of the stages, then there are some things you can do that will help you. When we accept Jesus it's like we are an embryo. As we grow spiritually, we become more mature and become something beautiful for God.

As I mentioned, there are things we need to do in order for this growth or transformation to take place. We are going to look at 10 things found in Psalm 119:9-16 that you can do to help you grow. The first thing I want to look at is in verse 9. "How can those who are young keep their way pure? By living according to your word." (Today's New International Version). When we think about the word living, we find it means, "The pursuit of a lifestyle of the specified type [18] You see, living for Jesus isn't just going to church once a week and calling it good. Instead, it's something you do every day, all the time. It's about having a relationship with Him, talking to Him, working with Him and for Him. It's about being quiet and listening for His voice.

When you are living with someone, there is give and take. You talk to them, you work with them on projects, you listen to them. There might be times you cry on their shoulder, or they might cry on yours.

God has given us a way to live close to Him. He has given us His Word. We can read it, meditate on it, memorize it, research it, and do our best to follow it. In other words, live according to what it says! You notice the first part of the verse says how someone young can stay pure. God is helping us out as much as possible.

This brings us to verse 10 which says, "I seek you with all my heart; do not let me stray from your commands."(TNIV). Don't you just hate it when you lose something? It's totally frustrating to look and look and not be able to find what you are looking for! The great thing about God though, is that when you seek Him, you will always find him!

Jeremiah 29:13-14 says, "You will seek me and find me when you seek me with all your heart. I will be found by you," declares the LORD."(TNIV). That is a promise God gives every one of us. We WILL find Him when we seek Him. He won't ever be lost. He is just waiting for us to come looking.

The next verse is verse 11. "I have hidden your word in my heart that I might not sin against you."(TNIV). God gives us the answer to the question of, "Why do I need to memorize scripture or read it every day?" His answer is, "That I might not sin against you." You know God is always working to help us get home. He is always ready and if we have scripture in our mind and heart, the Holy Spirit will bring it to our minds and help us when we need it.

There are lots of memory techniques out there. Just Google it and lots of things pop up. One of my favorite techniques is mnemonics. I like to use an acronym when I have a list of things to remember. An example of this would be for Philippians 4:8, "Finally, brothers and sisters, whatever is true, whatever is noble, whatever is right, whatever is pure, whatever is lovely, whatever is admirable, if anything is excellent or praiseworthy- think about such things."(TNIV). Here is the mnemonic I use.

T-true
R- Right
A- Admirable
P-Pure
P-Praiseworthy
L-Lovely
E-Excellent
N-Noble

TRAPPELN

It is a nonsense word, but it helps me remember this list of things that God has told me to think on when Satan comes bringing me trouble. Yes, the words are out of order, according to the way the verse is written, but I find that doesn't matter when I need to focus my mind on something other than a lie from Satan. I just start quoting this list sometimes out loud and other times in my head, but it works. I find myself focusing on Jesus and that's the whole point! Try it. You'll see, it works! You may need to find something that works for you, keep trying till you find just the right thing.

The next verse, verse 12 says, "Praise be to you, LORD; teach me your decrees."(TNIV). Here's my question to you: Are you teachable? I found several synonyms such as, "apt, eager, amenable, trainable, willing, bright and willing to learn."[19] John Maxwell says it means, "Having a passion to learn, possessing an intention to learn daily, and reflecting on what we're learning to know how to apply it."[20]

You see, it's one thing to read the Word, but if we are unwilling to apply it, or do what it says, there is not much point in reading it. We have to have a willing spirit and try our best to apply what is there.

Moving on to verse 13. "With my lips I recount all the laws that come from your mouth."(TNIV). There's that word, recount. Let's get a definition to start. In this verse it is used as a verb and it means "to tell someone about something."[21] That something that we are to be telling or recounting is all the laws that come from God's mouth. I'm thinking this is not only the do's and do not's in the Bible, but telling others what God is doing, or has done in your life.

Remember, all of these things we are looking at are helping us grow and change to become more like Jesus. There are a few more verses to check out, so let's keep going.

Verse 14 says, "I rejoice in following in your statutes as one rejoices in great riches."(TNIV). Have you ever seen someone who just won the lottery, or even a game show winner? Are they sad and mopey? Of course not! They just won a boatload of cash! Guess what? That's how happy we should be when we are following God's laws! We should be rejoicing, not walking around all sober and sad looking! There is no better place to be than in the direct will of God.

I'll tell you this COVID pandemic was hard on me in more ways than one, but one of the hardest things was the fact that we all had to wear masks! I know in the grand scheme of things that shouldn't have ranked high. If you lost a loved one or know someone who was really ill and may still be battling issues from it, this is in no way intended to be more important than that. But, let me tell you why it was hard for me. First, I like to smile at people when I see them. It breaks the ice and frankly, it makes me feel better. Secondly, I like to see other peoples faces so I can better assess what kind of day they may be having! If I can see that they are returning the smile I give, somehow that lifts my spirits. Also, if they are not returning the smile, I can tell that something is wrong and maybe they need help. So, you see, when all I could see was the eyes of people I met or saw in a store, I wasn't always able to get a sense of their well-being. I am a bit off topic here, but I want you to understand that our emotions show through our faces and our body language. If you are happy and rejoicing it should show on your face, you know, like you just won $1 million!

I like the way verse 15 reads: "I meditate on your precepts and consider your ways." (TNIV). Okay, back to the dictionary for meditate and consider. Meditate means to "silently calm or focus your mind for relaxation or spiritual reasons, to reflect deeply on a subject."[22] (Vocabulary.com). Consider means to "think carefully about something." (Oxford Dictionary)[23] This verse is helping us grow by telling us we need to focus on God's precepts. The word precepts means laws or rules. The rules and instructions given in the Bible are there for a reason. They teach us a good way to live, if we follow them. They will keep us out of trouble and help us have a civilized society. IF we will focus our minds and our hearts on God's Word we will be much better off.

One more verse. Verse 16 tells us, "I delight in your decrees; I will not neglect your word." (TNIV). Are you picking up on a theme from these verses? It seems the Psalmist is trying to get across that God's Word, the Bible, is pretty important. In this verse we are told to delight in His decrees, and to not neglect it.

If I delight in something I certainly don't neglect it. I delight in spending time with my daughter. I don't always get to be with her as much as I'd like, because we both have busy lives. I do, however, enjoy the times we are together all that much more. We do text almost every day, so I'm not neglecting this relationship and neither is she.

If we are really serious and wanting to grow and change in our relationship with Jesus, we must enjoy spending time in His presence. Everything discussed in this chapter should help you do that.

Here's the short list of what we've discussed.
Ten ways to grow closer to God:

1. Live according to His Word
2. Seek Him with all your heart
3. Hide His Word in your heart
4. Be teachable
5. Recount his laws
6. Rejoice in his statutes
7. Meditate on his precepts
8. Consider His ways
9. Delight in His decrees
10. Do not neglect His Word

Try these out if you are wanting "A Change" in your life. Trust God to be on the other end.

You have given me the capacity to learn. Teach me Your ways, oh Lord. I am listening for your instruction for my life. I desire to change in order that I may be more like Your Son, Jesus. You have placed great riches before me. Open my eyes that I may see. Lord, place Your Word in my heart and in my mind. Teach me to focus on You and the life You want from me. Teach me to rejoice and delight in Your Word daily.

In Your blessed Name!

Amen.

Chapter 5

God Loves You So Much

"Somehow you must come to understand that God is love, that love is the proof of God, and forgiveness is the proof of love."[24] When I first read that quote, I had to stop and go back and read it again and really think about it.

God is love, love is the proof of God and forgiveness is the proof of love. So, God is proved by His love and without God in our world bringing us love, we would have nothing, be nothing. He gave us proof of His love by giving us Jesus. Jesus' death on the cross, taking on your sin and mine too, is proof that God loves you more than you know or can even imagine.

Do you know how much God loves you? I mean really, loves you! In fact, He's crazy about you! He does everything in His power to show us that, but somehow, we miss it, don't we?

If you've read the book, "The Shack", then you know the author, Wm. Paul Young, uses the phrase when God is speaking, "I'm especially fond of him."[25] I love that! Just to think that God feels that way about you, about me, about everyone. I think if we can just grasp this idea, it will rock our world! When Mack the main character of the book asks God, "Are there any you are not especially fond of?" The answer was, "Nope, I haven't been able to find any!"[25] Amazing to think that God loves everyone and everything He ever created.

So, what makes God love us so much? Is it what we do for Him? It is because we are good enough? Is it because we are saved, born again? What is it that makes God love us and delight in us? Because He does delight in us you know!

Since we are made in His image and we have emotions, it must mean that God does too! I want to look at some of these emotions a little deeper (and see if we can learn what brings those emotions out of God).

Of course, in our lives and culture when you say emotions people tend to go to the negative ones first when they think of God. Why is that? Is it because we don't really know Him, and we don't know how much He really does love us? Because we don't know His heart? I think so! For the purposes of this lesson, I'd like to focus on the positive emotions.

The first emotion of God I'd like to explore is one I mentioned previously and that is delight. Psalm 147:11 says "The LORD delights in those who fear him, who put their hope in his unfailing love."(NIV). The type of fear being talked about here is a reverence, a deep respect. We are not talking about being scared of God because we think He is going to strike us dead with a lightning bolt. We are talking about being in awe of Him. Treating Him like the King that He is. When you honor God with your life, that makes Him delighted. It gives him great pleasure to know that you love Him and honor and respect Him.

Another verse about God delighting in us, is Psalm 149:4, "For the LORD takes delight in his people; he crowns the humble with victory."(NIV). In Today's New International Version Study Bible, it says in the footnotes, "He crowns us, or endows us with splendor." In other words, He wants to give us good things! Great things!

Queen Elizabeth II has been in the news lately as I'm writing this, because of her death. One thing that caught my attention was the crown on her coffin. It was beautiful in royal purple. "It had 2,868 diamonds, 17 sapphires, 11 emeralds, four rubies, and 269 pearls. It weighs over 1 kilogram (over 2.2 pounds)!"[26] Now that's what I call splendor! It is definitely over the top! That's what God wants to give us if we are humble and admit that we need Him every day, every moment. It doesn't mean that we will be rich and have a crown, necessarily, because God has so many other ways to bless our lives.

Another emotion that God feels is joy. Did you know that God rejoices over you with singing? He has a song just for you! I love that. Here is the verse that goes with rejoicing. Zephaniah 3:17, "The LORD your God is with you, the Mighty Warrior who saves. He will take great delight in you; in his love he will no longer rebuke you, but will rejoice over you with singing!"(TNIV). This verse actually is a three-promise verse! He will love, delight and rejoice over you. This has become a favorite verse for me. I love the picture I get of a Mighty Warrior fighting my battles for me. He loves me so much He fights for me and for you too. Then, because we love Him, He takes pleasure in us and feels great joy. So much so, that He sings over us!

When our girls were little their dad would sing "their" song. It was made up of a tune they were familiar with, but somewhere in that song their name was sung. They knew that Daddy was singing their own personal song. They loved that! It was special, it was all theirs and they knew it! I would love to hear my own personal song from the Lord, but for now, I have to settle for being blessed by the songs that others write.

There are a few places in the Bible where it tells us that God is pleased. This is the next emotion we want to look at. First Kings 3:4-13, shows God asking Solomon in a dream what he wanted and Solomon answered that he wanted, "A discerning heart, or a hearing heart with which to govern his people and to distinguish right from wrong."(TNIV). This in turn pleased God and He gave Solomon a wise and discerning heart. He blessed Solomon with more wisdom than any other person of his time, and along with that gave him great wealth and honor.

Another example of God being pleased with someone is in the New Testament. Matthew 3:17 says, "And a voice from heaven said, "this is my Son, whom I love, with him I am well pleased."(TNIV). Again, using my TNIV Study Bible I find that, "The tense of the Greek verb used here is timeless. God has always been and always will be 'well pleased' with his Son." This was recorded in two of the other gospels as well, in Mark 1:11 and Luke 3:22.

The last emotion I want to discuss will take the longest and require the most understanding. It will take us back to the beginning of this chapter. Remember the question I asked? You know the one. Do you know how much God loves you? Really loves you? Love is such a strong emotion. The dictionary definition of love is, "An intense feeling of deep affection."[27]

One of the best things I ever read about God's love was from Max Lucado. In his book, "In the Eye of the Storm," he recounts a conversation between God and an angel. It's all about the creation scene. You know, when God chose to create the earth and all who were to be in it. The first few creation days went along pretty smoothly. God has lots of imagination and we reap the benefits of that by being able to see and hear and taste and smell and enjoy His expressions of nature.

The part of this story that caught my attention though was when God decided to create human beings. He created us with a "seed, called choice." All of nature, all of the universe, everything He created was meant to worship Him and obey Him and reflect Him.

But only man was given a choice whether they would love Him and serve Him or not! He knew there would be some who would love Him and try their very hardest to show Him how much they love Him. He also knew there would be some who would reject Him. Some would forget that He even existed or tried to explain away His very existence.

As the story unfolds it shows a stable with a baby, then further along a cross on a hillside, where God's only Son hung. All of heaven was ready to go and rescue Him, but God stepped back with the words, "But it wouldn't be love."[28]

You see, He has given us a choice. If we had no choice but to serve Him and work for Him we would be no better than a robot. We would be resentful because we had no freedom, no choice.

Since God has given us this choice, we can be free to serve Him or not. When we don't, we break His heart. After all, He gave His Son for our souls. It makes Him sad, but He still loves us. When we do serve Him, it makes Him happy! He loves us so much He sent Jesus to die for us. Jesus accepted the sin and rejection of every single person who has ever lived because of God's love for us.

God knew all of this even as He created and formed the first body, but He did it anyway! He knew some would love Him and some would reject Him, but He has given everyone of us that choice. It doesn't matter whether you accept Him or reject Him, He still loves you. It doesn't matter what you've done, He still loves you. It doesn't matter what has been done to you, He still, still, still, loves you! He's always working, always trying, always reaching out to help bring you back to Himself! He loves you lots! He is crazy about YOU!

God of love, teach me the love You have shown to Your children. Thank You for loving me and placing Your word in song over me. As I go through my tasks today, may I take time to worship, obey and reflect on You. May Your love reach down and surround us in times of blessing and most of all in times we are hurting.

Your Love has lifted me! Amen.

And Know

Chapter 1

What do I need to know about Jesus?

I was going to start out this section with talking about Jesus, then I had the thought that the rest of Psalm 46:10 says, "And know that I am God." But that brought me back to Jesus because in John 14:7 Jesus says, "If you had known Me, you would have known My Father also; and from now on you know Him and have seen Him." (New King James Version).

There are a lot of "know" words in that verse. So, of course we have to look up the definition of the word "know." First off, the word "know" is a verb, that means there is an action involved. The first definition given was, "to be aware of through observation, inquiry, or information."[29] This reminds me of how we are before we become a Christian. We are observing others, becoming aware that they are somehow different. We might even ask a Christian some questions trying to gain information or understanding. We are becoming aware that maybe there is more to life than what we have.

The second definition, however, makes me think of someone who has accepted Jesus and is trying to live for Him. Here is what I found when I looked at the second meaning. To "have developed a relationship with (someone) through meeting and spending time with them; be familiar or friendly with."[29]

Wow! Now think back to the verse that was quoted in John 14:7. Jesus is saying that if we know Him (Jesus) that we should develop a relationship with Him. We should spend time with Him.

Why? Because when we do that, we get to know our Father God as well! I have to tell you that excites me! So, after going there in my head, I think we have to look at the life of Jesus! I'm going to try to answer the question asked in the title of this chapter. What do I need to know about Jesus?

There are volumes written about Jesus of course, but we are just going to look at a few things. First of all, we must start with who Jesus is. He is God's Son, the first born, God's only Son. In case you didn't catch it, that makes Him pretty important and special. You see, Jesus has been there since the beginning of time as we know it. Because of this fact, He is fully divine. He is the Son of the Only God. We will come back to this a bit later in the chapter.

Max Lucado explains the humanity and divinity of Christ really well in his book 'Unshakable Hope.' "Jesus was miraculously conceived, yet naturally delivered. He was born, yet born of a virgin. Had Jesus simply descended to earth in the form of a mighty being, we would respect him, but never draw near to him. After all, how could God understand what it means to be human?"[30] I find this fact about Jesus, the fact that He became fully human, to be helpful to me when I'm struggling with issues in life. Like you know, when I have a toothache, I wonder if Jesus felt aches and pains like we do? I think he must have. Don't you? Did He ever stub His toe or hit His thumb with a hammer? He must have! He was after all, human.

Okay, back to Max Lucado, "Had Jesus been biologically conceived with two earthly parents, we would draw near to him, but would we want to worship him? After all, he would be no different than you and me." If this were the case, what would be the point of worship? We could just choose any old person or someone famous to worship. There's a lot of that going on in our world today!

But Max goes on to say this and I love it! "But if Jesus was both - God and man at the same time - then we have the best of both worlds. Neither his humanity nor deity compromised. He was fully human. He was fully divine. Because of the first we draw near. Because of the latter, we worship." I know it can be hard for us to wrap our minds around the fact that He was fully both human and divine, but it's also a comfort to me to know that Jesus gets me! He totally understands my heart and my thinking and the way I react to situations. Thank God He came and lived here. Thank God He lives in heaven and talks to God for us!

In the next part of this chapter, I want to look at some pieces of Jesus' life while He was here on earth. I think there are some character traits we can learn from when we examine Jesus' life.

The first trait I want to look at is His kindness. Jesus was kind to women, children, the poor, and rich alike. How many examples can you think of for each of these sets of people? There are a lot, but a few stand out.

One amazing story is about the woman caught in the act of adultery. In this story in John 7:53-8:11, we see Jesus' kindness in the way He treated this wayward woman. He knew her life, He knew her story and what brought her to the place she was currently in, and instead of siding with the Pharisees, He chose to be kind to her. He could have ridiculed her along with those who had brought her to be stoned, but He could see through the deception of the Pharisees and saw through to the heart of the woman. If you are familiar with the story, you know that Jesus just stooped down and started writing in the dirt. We don't know what He was writing but we do know it was enough to stop the Pharisees holding rocks from throwing them. It was enough, in fact, to send them away one by one until the only two left were Jesus and the woman. Jesus knew about her, He knew her life, and yet told her He wouldn't condemn her. He didn't leave her in her sin though, He told her to go and leave her life of sin. Can you imagine the thoughts running through her head? She had just escaped death! She had just been set free! She had just been pardoned by the Master! Wow!

Some other acts of kindness on Jesus' part happened when the disciples tried to shoo the children away from Him. Jesus told them to let the kids come to him. I'm sure he got a kick out of playing games with them and laughing at the silly things they said, just like we do with our own little ones and our grandchildren.

We know Jesus was kind to the sick. He healed hundreds of people, from ones who were blind, to those who couldn't walk. Not only did He heal them, but in His kindness, He sought some of them out. We see the story in John 5:1-14 of the man at the Pool of Bethesda. This poor man had been lame a long time and had been trying to get to the waters when they were stirred. He believed there was restorative power in the water, not realizing that Jesus was the ultimate healer. When Jesus saw the man lying there, He asked him if he wanted to get well. The man told Him he had no one to help him to get to the pool, so he could never get there in time. Jesus told him, "Get up! Pick up your mat and walk!" The man did just that and he was healed! Amazing! Do you see the divine part of Jesus coming out in these healings? Who else was able to do these amazing things?

Jesus was also strong. I'm not talking about physically strong, although I'm sure He probably was. I'm referring to Him being strong in Spirit. After all, He cast out demons and when He was tempted in the wilderness, He put Satan in his place. He had the power to calm storms, and the power to raise the dead. He took on the Pharisees and walked on water! If He weren't the Son of God, in other words divine, He would not have been able to stand against all of these things or have mastery over them.

Not only was He kind and strong, but He was also smart. Think about all those parables He told. All of them related to something the people were familiar with, and told a truth they needed to hear. He was also a preacher bringing the Good News to people who had gone away from God. He taught people how to pray, and how to live a blessed life. But most of all I believe He showed us how to love. Who else but someone who had lived with the Father in heaven would have been able to be so astute?

That brings me to the end of the chapter and my final point. Jesus was loving. One of the things He did to show His love was feeding the large groups of people who had come to Hear him speak. He could have just as easily told them all to go home and feed themselves, but He felt compassion on them. They were hungry and had a long way to travel to reach home, so He took care of them. I know many times in my own personal life Jesus has given me what I needed when I needed it most. His grace comes to mind, but that is a whole other book!

Another example of His love was when He cried because Lazarus, his friend, had passed away. Even though Jesus knew that God would raise Lazarus up again, He still cried. I think Jesus also felt love for the city of Jerusalem. In Luke 13:34, He says that, "He has longed to gather the children together, as a hen gathers her chicks under her wings." In other words, He longs to protect her. We always want to protect the people we love, don't we? I believe Jesus still protects us today, probably in more ways than we can even imagine. There are so many more examples in God's Word about how much Jesus loved, but the ultimate is the last thing I want to finish this chapter with.

You've probably guessed by now, but I believe His greatest act of love was when He chose to die for me and you! He didn't have to do that, you know? He could have decided He just wanted to go back to heaven and live with His Father forever and be happy. But... He didn't do that. He came for a purpose. A divine purpose. He came here to earth knowing that He was to be our sacrifice. He was going to be put to death, so that we wouldn't have to be. My goodness, how awesome is that? It's hard for me to even express to you the magnitude of that love for me as an individual. But it wasn't just for me, it was for every single one of us! Every. Single. One. He loved us so much that He took every one of my sins, and every one of your sins and the sins of every single person on this planet who ever was, who ever is, and who ever will be, and died for each and everyone of us.

I heard an illustration recently that I just have to interject here. It's a three-part picture that I want you to try to get a hold of in your head. The first picture is of Jesus coming into our world much like a painter might enter his painting and become a character in that world. Can you imagine that? The second is a bit more down to earth, but could you see a farmer becoming an ear of corn? How about a shepherd becoming a sheep? You see, that's what Jesus did for us! He entered our world from His place in heaven and became one of us! Why did He do that? Because He loves us that much!

When Jesus died on that cross, He wiped all those sins completely out for us. Now, when we come to Him and ask for forgiveness, He casts them so far away we never have to see them again! Hallelujah!

Now, you might be thinking, if Jesus died, how is He able to do this forgiving thing? That's an even better part of this whole plan and shows His divinity really well. We know Jesus died on the cross, but we also know He rose again on the third day! He walked out of that tomb whole and alive. You see, He isn't a dead, moldy God lying in a tomb somewhere. He is alive! He is living, breathing, and still in love with us! He is sitting at the right hand of His Father, our Father God, and talking to Him about us right now. The really cool part is that we will get to go there too, someday if we take the time to get to "know" Him. How awesome is that? God made a way for us to know Him where there seemed to be no way! Praise God!

Oh Jesus,

How well you know me and watch over me. You know me personally down to the very hairs on my head. Lord, I am in awe that I have been given a personal invitation to get to know Your Son. I know love because Jesus showed me how to love. I know it is of You to show tears for Jesus wept.

Thank You for showing me that I am not better or no more unworthy of being cared for than anyone that does not know You. May Your Son be real to me in all that I think and do.

In Your loving name.

Amen.

Chapter 2

Why Jesus?

It dawned on me today that I have written all of this book to this point under the assumption that you, the reader, believes in God. That you believe that the Bible was written by men who were inspired by God. But what if that weren't the case? What if you didn't know anything about the Bible or Jesus or God? What then? Well, my thought is that you need to be introduced to them. That is what I'd like to do in this chapter.

Before I go into that introduction, I have to explain that my thoughts kept coming back to that question. That question of how and where, if a person isn't raised in a Christian home where they are taught about Jesus and the Bible, how and where do they get that foundation? How do they come to understand that the Bible is true and that Jesus is who He said he is?

I actually asked that question in my Bible study class knowing that there were several who didn't come from Christian backgrounds. I got great answers from them. Almost everyone of them said in one form or another that God's Spirit drew them, either through someone or with a desire put in their heart.

So, as I thought about that it took me to a lesson I taught on grace. The first type of grace I taught about was called prevenient grace, which basically means that God is wooing us or drawing us, pursuing us. He is making us aware of Himself. He is showing us that He is there, that He loves us and cares for us. You see He is building that foundation for us brick by brick. Jesus' Spirit is helping you and making you aware that you need Him. I just think this is the most amazing thing! I believe God will put people in your path who will help you see Him as well. I think things happen to us either positively or negatively that can have an influence on us.

My brother Mike was an awesome guy and I loved him dearly, but he told me once that if he hadn't gotten cancer he never would have come to God. Happily, he did come to know Jesus and lived out the last few years of his life as a Christian. Sometimes it takes something that drastic, but sometimes it doesn't.

Sometimes, the care and sacrifice of someone else is enough to help you find Him. Do you know someone who is living for Jesus? Is there someone in your life who cares about you and talks to you about Jesus or helps you out when you need a hand? In the MSG Bible, Ephesians 3:20-21 says, "God can do anything, you know-far more than you could ever imagine or guess or request in your wildest dreams. He does it not by pushing us around but by working within us, his Spirit deeply and gently within us." The Message Bible). I love that! Someone once told me, God is a gentleman, He will not push you into anything.

So, now we know that God is helping us even before we realize what we need. Let's look at Jesus' life and see what we can take from His life here on earth. There is a verse in 1 Timothy 3:16 that says: "Beyond all question, the mystery of godliness is great: He appeared in a body, was vindicated by the Spirit, was seen by angels, was preached among the nations, was believed on in the world, and was taken up in glory."(NIV).

Why Jesus? Why do we believe in Him and not one of the other gods from the multitude of religions out there? I think if we pick this verse apart, with the foundation that God's Word is true, we will find the answer to these questions. So, here we go!

We're going to start long before Jesus was even born into our world. There was a prophecy in Isaiah 9:6 that reads, "For unto us a child is born, to us a son is given and the government shall be upon his shoulders. And he will be called Wonderful Counselor, Mighty God, Everlasting Father, Prince of Peace." (NIV). This is just one of the many Messianic prophecies of Jesus. That means that a prophet said Jesus would be coming and when He did come, He would make that prophecy come true! "Mathematician Peter Stoner counted the probability of one person fulfilling even a small number of the prophesies about Jesus. And he concluded that a single man fulfilling "just" 48 of these prophecies found in the Tanakh (Old Testament) would be one in (10 followed by 157 zeros)!"[31] It has been noted that Jesus actually fulfilled 324 individual prophecies. So, we're off to a good start with our introduction to why we should believe in Jesus!

The next part of that verse from 1 Timothy says, Jesus appeared in a body. Most everyone knows the Christmas story. In Matthew and Luke, we see Mary giving birth to a son and He was named Jesus. The shepherds came and worshipped Him at his birth and the Magi came and worshipped Him at a little later stage in his life. Lots of people saw Him in his 33 years of life. They interacted with Him, ate with Him, laughed and cried with Him. I could go on and on, but you get the picture. He had a bodily form. People saw Him and eye witnessed Him. They knew He was real.

Moving on to the next part of the verse it says that Jesus was "vindicated by the Spirit." The word vindicated means, "to maintain, uphold or defend. To lay claim to or establish possession of."[32] God in His wisdom knew that we humans would need some proof of who Jesus was so He gave three of the four gospel writers a person they could talk to about this and the ability to get it written down. John 1:32-34 says, "I saw the Spirit come down from heaven as a dove and remain on him."(TNIV). John actually saw this. In verse 33 He goes on, "And I myself did not know him, but the One (God) who sent me to baptize with water told me, 'The man on whom you see the Spirit come down and remain is the one who will baptize with the Holy Spirit." You see, John the Baptist was able to see the Spirit of God come down in the physical form of a dove. He was able to vindicate or uphold by evidence of the dove descending that Jesus was, as verse 34 puts it, God's Chosen One. Matthew 3:16 and Mark 1:10 also give this same account of Jesus' baptism. These three accounts were of a physical nature, but Romans 8:16 says that, "The Spirit himself testifies with our spirit that we are God's children." (TNIV). Isn't it amazing that God has given us His Holy Spirit to live in our hearts and we can know beyond any doubt that He is who He says He is? I love that!

One to the next part of our verse! He "Jesus" was seen by angels. In Matthew 4:11 angels came and attended to Jesus' needs after his temptation time in the wilderness. He was hungry and tired and they took care of Him, not only physically but I'm sure there was some emotional support in the form of praising Him going on as well.

This wasn't the only time Jesus was seen by angels though. Three gospel writers tell the story of His resurrection. You know, where the stone was rolled away from the tomb where His body was laid! Angels were a part of all three accounts in Matthew 28:2-7, Mark 16:5-6 and John 20: 12-14. These angels were again part of the action! The verses in John tell us that Mary actually talked to them, then when she turned around, she saw Jesus standing there, so we know the angels must have seen Him too! These accounts are pretty important in my opinion because you see, the angels would have known Jesus when He was in Heaven. They knew who He was and for them to help Him and acknowledge Him while He was here on earth was an amazing proof for us that Jesus is God's Son! Just amazing!

The next part of our Timothy scripture says, "He was preached among the nations." The entire book of Acts in the Bible is a testament of Jesus being preached throughout the nations or world. Mark 16:20 tells us that the disciples went out and preached everywhere and that God worked with them and confirmed His word by the signs that accompanied it. Once Jesus was taken back up to heaven those disciples got busy! Because of the zeal they had for God, you and I are able to come to Him as well, and I don't live anywhere near the Middle East! Not only that, I got saved in a church just outside of a town called Nelsonville in Ohio. You see, God was spreading His message even to a little country church through some godly man preaching among the nations. I'm sure glad someone did, so I could hear the Good News!

We are not quite finished with the verse yet. The next part is, "He was believed on in the world." Again we need to look at the book of Acts. Chapter 4:4 says, "Many who heard the message believed," and there were about 5,000 who came to Jesus!"(TNIV). Romans 10:13 says, "Everyone who calls on the name of the Lord will be saved."(TNIV). Not, may be saved, but WILL BE saved. I"ll write more on that later.

Because of people like Paul, John, Peter, Titus and Timothy, churches grew in places like Corinth, Galatia, Colosse and Ephesis! So, can we say Jesus was believed on in the world? Oh, my yes! He is still being preached and believed on in our world today. Just look up Billy Graham and see how many people came to the Lord under his ministry. Our local churches are hopefully seeing people saved as well.

Last but not least, our verse in Timothy says, "He was taken up in glory." Let's go back to Mark 16:19, where it tells us that "Jesus was taken up into heaven, where He sits at the right hand of God." (TNIV). One commentator says, "He sat at the right hand of God, which denotes His sovereign dignity and universal power. He had finished His work on earth and now He appears before God as our Mediator. He has been where we are. He has suffered the same temptations we have suffered. And now He is in heaven still working on our behalf!"[33] What a great Savior we have on our side!

I know this all got a bit heavy, and I hope you made your way through it. I just want to look at the verse as a whole one more time.

"Beyond all question, the mystery of godliness is great: He appeared in a body, was vindicated by the Spirit, was seen by angels, was preached among the nations, was believed on in the world, was taken up in glory."

Can you see now, all the proof that God has given us so we can know Jesus? I pray your eyes are open to the truth.

Gracious God,

I have chosen You, through Jesus, to be my supplier of grace. You have extended grace to me and I have been saved. As I walk through life on this earth, help me to comprehend Your grace more and more in my life. Your love is amazing. Thank You for an unquestionable foundation in Your Word that God's Word is true.

Help me to put Jesus first in my daily living. You sent your Son to earth in order to prove to sinners like me the evidence of the Spirit, who carries and intercedes each prayer directly to You.

We ask, "Why Jesus?" You knew this was the only way we could see Your light. All blessings come from You! In Jesus precious name.

Amen.

Chapter 3

How do I get to Know Jesus?

In the last chapter I touched on the subject of prevenient grace. Again, this is God working in your life before you even realize that you need Him. He actually thought about you before you were even born. He made this plan available to every person on earth. It's really a pretty simple plan and it all begins with God's grace.

John Wesley preached a sermon a long time ago on grace. In it he talked about prevenient grace. That word prevenient means "preceding in time order."[34] In other words, this type of grace needs to happen before anything else. In the lesson I taught about grace I followed Wesley's thinking in his sermon and embellished on it just a bit. He talked about a front porch scene. I want you to think about a beautifully decorated front porch in the fall of the year. Can you picture it in your mind? Maybe there are some pretty mums in yellows and oranges. How about adding some pumpkins or gourds? Throw in a welcome sign and maybe a rocking chair or two! You getting a nice picture yet? I hope so, because I want you to understand how inviting this porch is. Maybe you can even see some lights on in the window. At any rate it all looks very comfy and homey!

You might think to yourself that this would be a great place to sit and visit. You might even decide you might like to stay awhile.

Now, I need you to take this porch scene and equate it with your life. You know that someone spent some time making that porch look like it did. Someone cared enough to decorate and make it look like a place where you would be welcome.

I hope and pray there is someone in your life who is making you feel special. That is making you feel like God loves you. You see, this doesn't have to just be on the porch, or at church, but this can take place anywhere. God's Holy Spirit is always working. He is there in your heart, speaking, drawing, helping you realize how much you need God. He is meeting you there on that porch of your life.

John 6:44 says that, "No one can come to me, unless the Father who sent me draws him."(TNIV). This means that you can't come to Jesus unless God gets your attention and helps you realize you need Him! Another verse that is important is 2 Peter 3:9, because the last verse left the question, 'If God doesn't do that for me, then what?' This verse says, "Not wishing that ANY should perish but that all should reach repentance."(TNIV). You see, God doesn't want you hanging out there all alone on that front porch! He wants you in His presence and living the life he intended you to have. This is why prevenient grace is so important. It's God's way of helping us get where we need to go.

Earlier I mentioned that I hope that you have someone in your life who is helping you, leading you to God. This is one way to experience this grace. Another way might be something that has happened in your life. It could be something positive or something negative. It might be that a neighbor thinks enough of you to bring you some cookies or helps you cut wood or any other number of things. It may be your local church having a VBS for your children or even someone smiling at you at the grocery story, just when you needed it! See, the Holy Spirit can speak in so many different ways. He knows just what you need when you need it. He's very inviting, just like our beautiful front porch at the beginning of our chapter.

So, once we understand that God is trying to get our attention, then what? Let's go back to the front porch. We might start to wonder what the inside of this house might look like. Is it pretty?

I would guess it's beautifully decorated as well. Will I be welcome to come and stay? Am I going to like it here? Will I need to work while I'm here? Should I wash up and get clean before I go in? I sure do have a lot of questions, but it's OK because God is there and He has the answers!

Think about that physical porch again. There is a door there just waiting for you. At this point you have a choice to make. Do I go or do I stay? Do I enter this house or walk away? We all, everyone of us have to make this choice. This leads us to the second type of grace I want to discuss, and that is justifying grace.

I want you to think about how you feel at this point? Are you afraid to enter? Are you excited? After all, this doorway could change your whole life! If you step into that entrance you will get to see the inside, you'll become more than just a visitor on the front stoop. If you don't go in, what will you be missing? Will there be people there you will like? You might never know what the inside looks like and that would be awful if you are a curious person like myself!

You know you can't stand with one foot inside and one foot outside forever. You have to make the decision, in or out? It's like sitting straddle a fence. The problem is, if you don't go one way or the other, you end up with splinters!

Alright, let's look now at the spiritual side of justifying grace. On our front porch you will notice there is only one door! This is the only way to get in this house. John 14:6 says, "I (Jesus) am the way, the truth and the life, that no one can come to the Father except through Me."(TNIV). If that isn't enough, here's another verse: Titus 2:11 says, "For the grace of God has appeared, that offers salvation to ALL people."(TNIV).

I believe these verses show us that Jesus is the only way to get in this house. He is the doorway, if you will. There is a simple plan that I've been aware of for many years. You must repent, believe, confess and receive. Let's look at each one of these words.

Once you repent or decide that you want to go in, you must *turn* and go through the door. The word repent means, "to feel or express sincere regret or remorse about one's wrongdoing or sin."[35] You notice I used the word "turn". That's because if you truly repent and feel bad about your sin, you will turn around 180 degrees and go the other way! In other words, you will turn your back on that life of sin.

The next word is believe. If you read the previous chapter then I pray you do believe Jesus is who He says he is. Even the demons in Mark 1:24 recognized Jesus. Here is what the demon said, "What do you want with us, Jesus of Nazareth? Have you come to destroy us? I know who you are- the Holy One of God!"(NIV). I believe this is just another proof that Jesus is God's Son.

The definition of believe is, "to accept (something) as true."[36] This step to acquiring salvation is to believe that Jesus really is God's Son. He really did come to earth just for you and died just for you! Let that sink in to your soul.

The next step is to confess. By this point if you have realized that you need to turn from your sin and you believe that Jesus came for you, you are probably feeling some sadness about the life you've been living. Here's the cool thing about this part of confessing. If you just ask Jesus to forgive you for those sins, He will! It's really that simple! It doesn't matter what you've done. Remember the question you had on the porch? You know the one about washing up before you enter? Don't worry about that, because what Jesus did when He died on that cross and rose again three days later, took care of all that for you. He became your sacrifice and mine, for all those sins. What an amazing thing He did for us!

This leads us to the next word, which is "receive". To this point you have hopefully turned or repented of your sin, believe that Jesus is who He says he is and have confessed your sins to Him. The next thing is to receive Him. Ask Him to come into your heart and live in you, to help you through every day.

Think back to when you entered the front door. You are now able to see the inside. You don't have to wonder anymore what it looks like. You are no longer on the outside looking in. You and the Father are now on speaking terms!

I came across the term, "unflinching love" in regard to Jesus. You and He are now in a relationship because of His unflinching love. At the time I came across this term I wrote this next paragraph because it stuck out to me.

Jesus didn't flinch when they whipped Him, put a crown of thorns on His head, drove nails in His hands, stood that cross upright and let it fall in place. He didn't flinch when He hung on that cross being ridiculed by the crowds, and by the thief hanging beside him. He didn't flinch when He knew God His Father wasn't looking His direction because he had taken my sin on Himself. He didn't flinch when He took his last breath. Because He loves you and me so much, He didn't flinch. He didn't flinch.

Well, now that you've walked through the door of justifying grace, there is one more type of grace yet to talk about and that is sanctifying grace. If we go back to the house metaphor let's think about what that might look like.

When you step into someone's home you can tell a lot about them. You can tell what they are interested in by looking at how the house is decorated or by listening to them talk. You might see pictures on the wall or sitting in a prominent place. There might be seasonal decor. One thing you probably won't see though are signs telling you what each room is, or an exit sign, or signs on drawers telling you not to open. Signs are important to us in our every day life, but probably not so much in our homes.

We need signs or directions. I have to tell you about a trip I took. On this trip, I had a layover in Chicago, an airport that I'd never been to before. I'm not afraid to say I had a bit of fear and trepidation that I'd be able to navigate that airport. I'm happy to say, however, that the signage in the airport was awesome! As soon as I got off the plane, I could see a sign pointing me in the right direction. I did end up in the place I was supposed to be with time to spare!

So, by now I'm sure you know where I'm going with this! God in His infinite wisdom knew that we would need a guidebook, or signs if you will, and He provided it for us with this type of grace. Not only is this grace called sanctifying grace, but it could also be called sustaining grace.

God has given us His Word, the Bible, to point us in the right direction. There have been probably millions of books written about the Bible. God has placed this physical item in our hands to help us! If we read the Word and listen to its wisdom and guidance, we will know which way to go.

He has also given us His Holy Spirit. If we have stepped over the thresh hold and into the life, He wants to give us, then we have His sustaining Spirit in us. This sustaining Spirit helps us through each and every day, hour and moment.

In Gwen Smith's book, "I Want it All," she talks about working out the kinks of our circumstances and relationships with others and with God. She says:

1. "We are now acquainted with the Father of the house and we can ask Him for grace and help instead of depending on our own strength.
2. We can go to Him in prayer.
3. We can align our life and choices we make to His Word.
4. We can yield to His Holy Spirit."[37]

We need God's grace! Whether it be prevenient grace that draws us to Him in the first place, or justifying grace that allows us to accept Him or sanctifying grace that helps us continue to live for him. We need grace. God has provided everything we need so we can go home and be with Him forever when our end comes! What a comforting thought! God is good, all the time!

Oh Jesus,

Today and just now Lord, I want to acknowledge Your grace which You have given me. You have shown me how to accept and keep grace present in my daily walk with You. I see how my life has changed once I accepted Your invitation to enter through the door which is always open and calling me closer to a personal conversation with You. I owe my life to You for Jesus blood that has washed me clean and bright. When I make a wrong choice, Your grace is sufficient for me.

Amen.

Chapter 4

I've Accepted Jesus, What Now?

In our last chapter we read about three types of grace. I want to focus on the very last one in this chapter, sustaining grace or sanctifying grace.

The word sustaining means, "to strengthen or support physically or mentally."[38] The word sanctify means, "to set apart." I want you to understand that this is what God does for you after you have accepted Him. Here is where I want you to go back and read the first few chapters of this book again! I hope you will see that God has a way of helping us live for Him! Hopefully, you will be able to see that in the first few chapters.

One of the best and biggest things you can do is open your Bible. Rick Warren in "*The Purpose Driven Life*" says this, "The Spirit of God uses the Word of God to make us like the Son of God,"[39] and it's so true! We need God's Word to help us navigate through this life. That's what this entire book is all about! Get in the Bible and find out what is there. You will be amazed!

I made a list of some of the things that God's Word does for us. I'm certain there are lots more, but here are a few. God's Word creates faith, produces change, generates life, scares the devil, causes miracles, heals our hurts, changes our circumstances. It gives us joy and peace, helps us overcome troubles and trials, and helps us defeat temptation. It cleans up your mind, and reassures us that we can have eternal life. Wow! What an amazing list of things! If His Word can do all of that and more, I think we should get in there and read it.

Let's look a little more closely at the truth of God. His Word has been used as a metaphor for some different kinds of food. You know that if you don't eat real food, that you wouldn't be able to live long. It's the same way with the Word of God. If we don't get into it and find out what is there we won't last very long. So, what are some of the kinds of food? Well, the Word has been called milk. In 1 Peter 2:2 it says in the Amplified Bible, "Like newborn babies (you should) long for the pure milk of the word, so that by it you may be nurtured and grow in respect to salvation (it's ultimate fulfillment)." You see, when you first accept Jesus, you are like a baby. You're just learning all these new things. You need a guide book to help you gain knowledge and understanding. I would recommend that you read your Bible. I would also recommend that you find someone you know and trust as a Christian to become a mentor for you, to help you learn and grow and get your footing in this new life you've started!

Alright, you know that as a child grows, they can transition to other kinds of food. So, too, can you as you grow in being a Christian. Jesus said in John 6:35, "I am the Bread of life. Whoever comes to me will never go hungry and whoever believes in me will never be thirsty."(NIV). Obviously, Jesus was not talking about physical hunger and thirst here. He was talking about your spiritual state. He will fill you up and sustain you. There's that word "sustain" again. Just like when your stomach is empty and you eat bread you feel full, it's the same way with reading God's Word for your spiritual side. It will fill you up and keep you strengthened and supported. Isn't that what our definition of sustaining said?

Another category of food the Bible represents is "solid food." Again, just like a child, as they are growing, can transition from a soft food, so can you, move to something more solid like meat! As you grow and learn more about Jesus and the Bible you can take on more and more. Hebrews 5:14 says, "But solid food is for the mature, who by constant use have trained themselves to distinguish good from evil."(NIV). As you live life, you will find in God's word, the necessary mindset to be able to go in the right direction. Jesus will show you the way to live and help keep you from getting caught up in something that could be harmful to you. I just think this is the most awesome thing- to know that we have someone willing to be there for us, to keep us from falling or failing!

One last type of food before we move on. God's Word is like a sweet dessert! The good thing about this dessert though is that you won't get fat from eating too much of it! (Yeah!). In Psalm 119:103 it states, "How sweet are your words to my taste, sweeter than honey to my mouth."(NIV). Just like most of us, babies learn to enjoy sweets at a young age. You see, God's word is sweet. It instructs us, gives us hope, helps us see where to go. Shows us about Jesus, and has promises we can hold on to when life throws us curve balls, which I'm here to tell you, will happen!

So, how do you go about reading the Bible? Well, there are lots of Bible reading plans out there. If you Google the phrase, "Bible reading plans", you will get a whole list of possible plans. I've always heard you should start with the gospel of John in the New Testament. If you want to learn about Jesus, start in Matthew and go on through Mark, Luke and John. Sometimes there are lists of names there, but don't let those discourage you. Just skip them for now and later when you are ready for some meat you can come back to them. There is a reason they are there! The whole point here is to open the Bible and read.

What if you aren't a good reader though? Then I encourage you to look for a way to be able to hear the Word spoken. Apps are available to download that will read the Bible to you. There are podcasts, preachers, etc. Everyone who really wants to learn can find a way, especially with our current technology.

I've put together 5 R's that I've picked up along my journey. They are, Receive God's Word, Read it, Research it, Remember it, and Reflect on it.

The first R is receive God's word, listen to it and accept it with an open mind. Let it speak to you. If you are receptive and have the right attitude it will help you.

Next is read it. That's what we've been discussing. In Deuteronomy 17:19 even the kings in the Old Testament were to read the word and follow it! Read till God shows you a verse that stands out to you, then stop and really think about what it means. There are a ton of devotional books on the market that you can buy and there are lots of devotions found on line as well. Our Daily Bread is a good place to start or In Touch by Dr. Charles Stanley. Be sure to ask a trusted friend or your Pastor for recommendations. There could be some issues with devotional books, so be sure to check out what the Bible has to say first and foremost. It is our final authority!

Next comes research. Study the Bible, ask questions, keep a journal to write down things that stand out to you. There are Bible verse mapping plans that will help you break down a verse and even apply it to your life.

Remember is the next R. Memorize the verse. Let God show you a verse or give you a verse that is a promise and you will find it easier to commit to memory. I have found over the course of this last year that writing verses out helps me remember them better. Whatever technique works best for you, do it! The point is to internalize the Word, because you will need it at some point!

Last, but certainly not least, is to Reflect. Meditate on it, think about it. How does this verse help you? What promise has God given you? Which direction is He leading you?

Be aware that there are a lot of great devotional books out there. There are a lot of different books you can read. But, the very best book you can read is your Bible! God's Word is the best and final authority. Open it up and read it and let God speak to you personally! You won't be sorry.

I do want you to know however, that we have an adversary out there who will fight against you. His name is Satan, and he is always working to drag you down, which is another reason we need to get God's Word in our hearts and heads! He doesn't mind if you read the Word or go to Bible study as long as you don't do anything with what you've learned. Our God is greater though and He will always keep us safe.

I hope this chapter has helped you get started. I don't want to mislead you into thinking that all of this is easy as pie. It will take some effort on your part. The awesome thing though, is that God will come and meet you. He will help you. Remember the 5 R's, remember that you are just starting out and you can't learn everything there is to learn in a week, month or even a year! As a matter of fact it will take a lifetime and we still won't know everything there is to know about the Bible. It's O.K. though because God just wants us to take one day at a time!

Lord Jesus,

You are there for me. You hear not only my prayer of forgiveness and trusting in You for my every need, but You also know when and what I need to eat. Your Word feeds my spirit and inner being. May I put to use that which is given me to glorify You. I feel You walking beside me as the trials of life surround me. Be close now as I continue my walk, day by day and beside the One who keeps me from falling.

In Jesus name I pray.

Amen.

That I Am God

Chapter 1

God is Omniscient

"Tell them I love them, even though I know everything about them. I want them to know that nothing they do will turn me off or make me go away. I know what they are thinking. I know what they are doing. I know when they are angry, upset, depressed, in love, out of love. I know when they are sick, on vacation, or at the doctor's office. I know it all, and I love them!"

The above paragraph was written as I was praying about how to write this chapter. I had started with notes a few times and nothing was working. I decided to just stop and let God speak. And He did!

You see, God is Omniscient. He knows everything! He knows the past, the present and the future. He knows everything and everyone He ever created. He knows me better than I know myself.

Psalm 139:1-5 says this: "You have searched me, LORD, and you know me. You know when I sit and when I rise; you perceive my thoughts from afar. You discern my going out and my lying down; you are familiar with all my ways. Before a word is on my tongue you, LORD, know it completely. You hem me in behind and before and you lay your hand upon me."(NIV).

He knows it all. Does that comfort you? Does it make you feel good to know that God loves you enough to want to be involved in everything concerning you?

Think about this: You are fixing your family's favorite meal. You first go to the store and purchase the ingredients. You make sure to get just the right item because you know just what this meal should taste like. Once at home you start cooking using those ingredients you bought. You might add in a secret ingredient that pulls it all together and then it's ready to serve. The family gets a whiff of it and stomachs start to growl. They eat heartily and you are glad because you know what went into this meal. You know the time it took to prepare. You know the ingredients. You made this favorite meal because you love your family. You worked to make it the best for them.

Are you seeing the correlation here? God knows all about you. He created you. He used all the best ingredients to make you exactly who you are! He loves you, even though you may not love Him back (yet).

This is what Omniscience is all about. God knows what is going on in our lives. Sometimes we don't feel that way though. Sometimes we struggle with things that happen in our lives that don't make a whole lot of sense to us. You know what I'm talking about! Sometimes bad things happen in our lives that leave us wounded. Does God know about that too? Of course, He does.

An example from my own heart was when we lost our precious 20-year-old daughter in a car wreck. I was grieving and in shock when a friend from our church showed up. She had previously been through a similar thing when she unexpectedly lost her son a few years prior to this. Here's what I remember the most. Her only words to me were, "I know." In a strange and wonderful way, it comforted me to know that she really did know. She had been there and she knew exactly how I was feeling. You see, God knows exactly how you are feeling. He gets it.

Why, then, does God allow bad things to happen? The only answer I have been able to come up with is that we live in a broken world. Bad things are going to happen to all of us at some point. Because of sin in our world, we all end up suffering. Here's where the fact that God knows us is helpful. He knows our thoughts, our feelings, our shattered dreams and He is there to comfort us, to love us and help us out of the mess. I can tell you from personal experience that He will do just that.

God has a plan in His all knowingness (is that even a word?) for your life. He gave His Son, Jesus, so that we can have eternal life, so we can go and live with Him forever.

So, I'm okay with God being all-knowing. It helps me trust that whatever has happened, is happening, or will happen, is already known by God. He is filtering everything for me and not allowing anything that would pull me away from Him! Praise God! I need all the help He is willing to give!

Oh Jesus,

I am in awe that you could love me as You do. With all of my faults, when I get stressed and want to say unkind things. You know me better than I know myself. I am not proud of my past, but I understand You knew me then and knew what I was feeling. Forgive me Lord when I stray.

You have made me in Your image; therefore, I know you "get it." You know my strengths and my shortcomings. You are my stronghold, my comforter; may I never leave your side. Thank You for loving me as Your own. May my spirit yield to your omniscient way.

Amen.

Chapter 2

God is Omnipresent

Our God is Omniscient or all knowing, as we discussed in the last chapter, but He is also Omnipresent which means He is present everywhere! What a thought! I think its hard for us humans to really grasp what that means. I think it's made even harder because we can't physically see Him.

The thing is though, we can see the things He's done, things He's created and things He's doing right now. We just have to stop, be calm, and be still. That's what this book is about. Taking the time to be still and really hear from Him.

Because God is Omnipresent, He can be in your heart and my heart and every other believer's heart at the same time. That's what make Him special and THE only God. There has never been any other god, or person who thought they were God, who is still alive and well and moving in people's hearts.

It comforting to me to know that He is everywhere. Psalm 139:7-12 says: "Where can I flee from your presence? If I go up to the heavens, you are there; if I make my bed in the depths, you are there. If I rise on the wings of the dawn, if I settle on the far side of the sea, even there your hand will hold me fast. If I say, 'Surely, the darkness will hide me and light become night around me, even the darkness will not be dark to you; the night will shine like the day, for darkness is as light to you."(NIV).

You know that old saying, "You can run but you can't hide?" I feel like that's what these verses are saying! It doesn't matter where you go, what you do, who you are or who you are with. It doesn't matter if you run away or stay put, it just doesn't matter, because God is there. You can't outrun Him. You can't outwit Him and you can't outlast Him. He always was, always is, and always will be.

Verse 10 is why this all gives me comfort. Look at it again: "Even there your hand will guide me, your right hand will hold me fast." See, He is there, not to bring down wrath on you, but to love you and guide you and keep you from going off the rails and getting into trouble. He has a perfect plan for you and IF you will let Him, He will help you every step of the way. Does this mean that you are never going to do the wrong thing? Does this mean that you are never going to sin or make a mistake? Oh, my friends, NO it doesn't mean that at all! We are still human and we will still do things we shouldn't. However, God is forgiving and if we ask Him with a sincere heart to forgive us, He most certainly will.

I don't want you to think that it is alright for you to go out and do whatever you want because God will forgive you. That is certainly not what I'm saying! I believe if we are living for God and doing the very best, we know how, that He will bless us and help us, but we can't take advantage of that love for us.

I like this quote from C.S. Lewis, "We may ignore, but we can nowhere evade the presence of God. The world is crowded with Him. He walks everywhere incognito."[40] Look around folks, you never know when you will see Him!

This quote from A. W. Tozer is good too, "Always, everywhere God is present, and always He seeks to discover Himself to each one,"[41] God is looking for you. He wants you to become his child.

We must, everyone of us, meet God at some point and accept Him or reject Him. I pray you make the right choice. Look for Him in your day. You will find Him because He's everywhere!

Heavenly Father,

I feel Your presence with me Father. I can not imagine going anywhere or doing anything without You being by me and wrapped around me. Lord, take my hand, lead me where I need to go. Show me Your ways that I may fulfill my time on earth as You desire. Keep me from wrong and when I am in error, I ask for gentle hands to lead me back to You.

Amen.

Chapter 3

God is Omnipotent

The last chapter in this section is about God's omnipotence. This means He is all powerful. The Bible is full of stories of God's power. There were many to choose from so I just chose some of my favorites.

In following Psalm 139, like the previous chapters, let's look at verses 13-16. God is powerful enough to create us in such a way that we, as women, can procreate. Verse 13-16 says, "For you created my inmost being; you knit me together in my mother's womb. I praise you because I am fearfully and wonderfully made; your works are wonderful. My frame was not hidden from you. Your eyes saw my unformed body."(NIV). That was paraphrased a bit, but isn't it amazing that God has the ability and power to form us, a little human, inside another human? That is mind boggling! He knows what we are going to look like, what we're going to do, who we will be, before we are ever conceived!

I also love this next story. This one is found at the very beginning of the Bible. I find the story of creation to be one that shows God's power the most.

When I think about there being absolutely nothing, and then God speaks, and the earth was created, I am in awe. I know there are lots of theories out there that try to tell us how the earth was formed, but really is it so hard to believe in an all powerful Being who was able to speak it into existence? Or is it easier to believe that the "universe expanded from a single point and kept stretching?"[42]

(Big Bang Theory). I have no problem believing our God is powerful enough to make our world! Why, He could have even created that single expanding point if He wanted to!

You probably know the creation story pretty well! You know the second day light was created, then our atmosphere, which by the way, is exactly what we as humans need to be able to breathe. No other planet has an atmosphere like Earth. Not only that, but God put Earth just the right distance from the sun to keep us from being frozen or burned up!

God put vegetation on the dry ground, things that would also be good for us for food and oxygen. On day four He put the sun and moon and stars in the sky. I've recently been seeing lots of posts on Facebook from NASA and the James Webb Telescope. They are showing pictures of outer space that have never been seen before! There are some wonderfully spectacular things out there! On day five God created the ocean animals of which there are "240,000 different species."[43] On this day He also made the birds and I found that there are around "10,000 species of them."[44]

Day six was a pretty important day! On this day He created around "6.5 million species of land animals."[45] You've undoubtedly seen enough TV shows on animals to know how diverse they are. Why am I telling you all these numbers? I want to get you to think about how powerful God is to have created all of these things. His imagination is huge! The diversity of our Earth is amazing!

Not only did God create land animals on day six, but he also made man and woman. Adam and the animals were all formed from the earth, but Eve was formed using one of Adam's ribs. The best part was that everything about Adam and Eve and the animals and the earth was that everything was perfect. God the Creator of the universe and everything in it, did a good job! He didn't make any mistakes. He still doesn't. If you are wondering why you were born, or why things are the way they are in your life, it's because God want to work something wonderful in your life. It took Someone pretty powerful to create all of these things, animals and people from nothing, into this amazing world we live in.

Another Old Testament story that some of you are probably familiar with is the story of Moses and the ten plagues of Egypt. If you are, then you know that this is another story about God's power. He had to use His power here in this story to get Pharaoh to let His people, the Israelites, leave Egypt.

This story shows the power or omnipotence of God in all the different plagues that were brought on the Egyptian people. It's interesting that each one of the plagues was aimed at one of their gods, but that's a whole other story!

Exodus 7:14-11:10 is the reference point for this powerful display of God's strength. There was water turned into blood, a LOT of frogs, gnats or lice, flies, a plague that killed the livestock, boils on people and animals, hail that destroyed their crops, locusts to eat what was left from the hail, darkness so dark the people were like being blind and the worst plague of all was the death of the firstborn.

You see, Pharaoh just wouldn't relinquish his power. He wouldn't do what he was supposed to do. God showed His power over the gods of Egypt and eventually His people were asked to leave. What a story!

Another Old Testament story is one of my very favorites. Elijah was a prophet of God and he met with King Ahab. He tried to get Ahab to understand that he shouldn't be following the false gods called Baal and Asherah. He was leading the Israelites away from God as well, and Elijah was trying to get him to change his ways. This story is found in 1 Kings 18:16-40. It tells of a showdown between the 450 prophets of Baal and the 400 prophets of Asherah and Elijah on the other side as the one lone prophet of God!

Both sides were to bring a bull, cut it into pieces and lay it on wood to make a sacrifice to their gods or in Elijah's case to God. The only condition was that their respective gods/God would be the one to start the fire. If you know the story you know the prophets of Baal and Asherah prayed all day. Around noon Elijah started taunting them because nothing was happening! So, they prayed harder and louder and even started cutting themselves with swords, but nothing worked! Then Elijah steps up and asks that his pile of wood and the bull be doused in water. Not just one jar of water, but 12 large jugs of water! You can imagine how wet that wood must have been. There was so much water that the moat around the wood pile was filled with water!

Here's where the power of our God comes in. Elijah prayed and the fire of God fell and burned up the sacrifice, the wood, the stones, the soil and all the water in the moat!

Oh man! Those people were amazed! They had just spent an entire day watching their prophets entreat their gods to do something and in steps Elijah with one prayer and boom! Fire from heaven! Needless to say, he made believers out of them.

On to the next story. This one is from the New Testament. It has always been my favorite. It is the story about the woman who had the issue of blood for twelve years. This poor lady had been to doctor after doctor and had suffered from different treatments. She had also spent a lot of money on those treatments and had nothing to show for it. Bless her heart, she was desperate! I always liked the story because of the amount of faith she had. She just knew that if she only could touch His (Jesus') clothes that she would be alright. But I want you understand that God's power, through Jesus, even into the garment He had on, was what healed her. Jesus knew the exact moment that His power was released, but that sweet lady knew it too! Praise the Lord! I love that she was immediately healed through God's power!

The last show of God's power I want to discuss is His power over death. You probably know the story about Lazarus being raised from the dead. He had been in his grave four days when Jesus came and called him out! There is another story about Jesus being the One in the grave. He'd been there three days, when God used His power to bring Jesus out!

In our day and time people have been brought back from death after just a few minutes, but no one has been brought back after days! You see, it takes supernatural God power for things like that to occur.

I've only taken the time to write about just a small fraction of the Biblical stories about the power of God. If you start keeping track you will be amazed how many there are. I'm so thankful that my God is omnipotent. He is all powerful, and that means there is nothing too difficult for Him to do.

He is powerful, He is all present, and He is everywhere. Knowing all of this helps me grow and stay strong. He uses this power to help us find our way to heaven! Thank you, God!

Lord Jesus,

From the time I open my eyes I see You all around me. I see You in the sunrise and even in the clouds when skies are grey. Your power is within me. I am weak, but You alone, Lord, are strong. Please do not allow my imperfections to get in the way of seeing Your strength.

Bless me now as I walk with You and learn more about how I am to live under Your power.

Amen.

In Closing...

One last word to kind of tie all this together. It is my prayer that as you read, you are able to gain a better understanding of God and His perfection. I pray you can hear from God and that if you can find the stillness in your life to listen for His voice and follow His Word, you will be able to have a power - filled life as well. Our weakness is made perfect in Him. He brought that verse to me many times during the writing of this book. He is my Strength for everyday, every moment, and every second. I hope you will let Him be your Strength as well.

God is powerful but sometimes He comes in the stillness. Listen for Him. Love Him. Adore Him. You'll see.

BIBLIOGRAPHY

Power in Stillness

1. Dean Smith, "*The Divided Mind of Worry*," January 15, 2014.
2. TheFreeDictionary.com, s.v. "fret," accessed August 1, 2022, TheFreeDictionary.com.
3. Ibid.
4. Merriam - Webster Dictionary, s.v. "trust," accessed December 23, 2022, https://www.merriam-webster.com.
5. Merriam-Webster Dictionary, s.v. "cultivate," accessed December 12, 2022, https://www.merriam-webster.com.
6. Sarah Young. *Jesus Calling*. Nashville, Tennessee: Thomas Nelson, 2004.
7. Charles Stanley, In Touch Ministries, August 2, 2022, accessed December 12, 2022. www.intouch.org.
8. Word Reference House learner's Dictionary of English Language, s.v. "delight," accessed August 10, 2022, https://www.wordreference.com.
9. Thesaurus.plus, s.s. "Delight," accessed August 10, 2022, https://www.Thesaurus.plus.
10. "What is commitment?," Got Questions Ministries, accessed August 10, 2022, [https://www.gotquestions.org/what-is-cimmittment.html]
11. Oxford English Dictionary, s.v. "abide," accessed December 23, 2022, https://www.oed.com,
12. Ibid."Wait," accessed December 23, 2022.
13. U.S. Department of the Interior. Metamorphic Rock. Accessed August 22, 2022. https://www.usgs.gov.
14. Merriam - Webster Dictionary, s.v."perseverance," accessed August 23, 2022, https://www.merriam-webster.com.

15. Shirer, Priscilla. "Inside Information." In Book *Discerning the Voice of God, How to Recognize when God is Speaking*, edited by Pam Pugh, 47-48. Chicago, Illinois;Moody Publishers, 2012.

16. Sarah Young, *Jesus Always, Embracing Joy in His Presence*. Nashville, Tennessee: Thomas Nelson, 2016.

17. Gill, John. Gill's Exposition of the Entire Bible. Salem: Salem Web Network, Salem Media Group, 2022. https://www.Biblestudytools.com.

18. Oxford English Dictionary, s.v. "living,", accessed September 3, 2022, https://www.oed.com

19. Roget's 21st Century Thesaurus, s.v. "teachable," accessed September 3, 2022, https://www.thesaurus.com.

20. Maxwell, John. "If you want to grow, cultivate a teachable spirit." January 15, 2019. https://www.johnmaxwell.com>blog.

21. Oxford English Dictionary, s.v. "recount," accessed September 3, 2022, https://www.oed.com.

22. Vocabularycom, Inc, s.v. "meditate," accessed September 3, 2022, https://www.vocabulary.com.

23. Oxford English Dictionary, s.v. "consider," accessed September 3, 2022, https://www.oed.com

24. W.Dale Cramer, *Levi's Will.* Minneapolis, Minnesota: Bethany House, 2005.

25. Wm Paul Young, *The Shack, Where Tragedy Confronts Eternity.* Newbury Park, California: Windblown Media, 2007.

26. Sarah McDermott and Kirstie Brewer. "The Dazzling Crown which sat on the Queen's Coffin." September 2022. https://www.bbc.com.

27. Oxford English Dictionary, s.v. "love," accessed September 22, 2022, https://www.oed.com

28. Lucado, Max. "The Choice." In *In the Eye of the Storm*, 237-243. Dallas, Texas: Word Publishing, 1991.

29. Oxford English Dictionary, s.v. "know," accessed October 7, 2022, https://www.oed.com

30. Lucado, Max. "God Gets You." In *Unshakable Hope*, 71-72. Nashville, Tennessee: Harper Collins Christian Publishing, Inc. 2018.

31. Bernis, Jonathoan, "How Many Prophecies did Jesus Fulfill?" Messianic Bible Teaching. January 31, 2015. https://www.firmisrael.org.

32. Cambridge Advanced Learner's Dictionary, s.v. "vindicated," accessed December 29, 2022, https://www.dictionary.cambridge.org.

33. Henry, Matthew. "Mark 16:19." Matthew Henry's Complete Commentary on the Whole Bible, 1706, Bible Hub App. 2004-2022.

34. Oxford English Dictionary, s.v. "prevenient," accessed August 26, 2022, https://www.oed.com

35. Ibid. "repent".

36. Ibid. "believe".

37. Smith, Gwen. "Not Just a Prayer we say before Dinner." In , 46-47. Colorado Springs, Colorado: David C.Cook 2016.

38. Oxford English Dictionary, s.v. "sustaining," accessed November 4, 2022, https://www.oed.com

39. Warren, Rick. *Transformed by Truth*. Grand Rapids, Michigan: Zondervan, 2002. p185.

40. Caraballo, Sophia, "17 Best Quotes about God and His Wisdom," Womans day, July 11, 2022, C.S. Lewis, https://www.womansday.com

41. Ibid. A. W. Tozer.\

42. NASA. "What is the Big Bang Theory?" *NASA. March 17, 2021. https://www.spaceplace.nasa.gov.*

43. "World Register of Marine Species," WORMS 2022, https://www.marinespecies.org

44. *Rodewald P.G. and Schulenberg, T.S.,* "Birds of the World," The Cornell Lab of Ornithology, 2023,https://www.birdsoftheworld.org

45. Nowatschin, Jan. "Animals around the Globe," https://www.animalsaroundtheglobe.com.